Hotel Confidential

A MEMOIR

Guenter H. Richter

Hotel Confidential © copyright 2024 by Guenter H. Richter. All rights reserved. No part of this book may be reproduced in any form whatsoever, by photography or xerography or by any other means, by broadcast or transmission, by translation into any kind of language, nor by recording electronically or otherwise, without permission in writing from the author, except by a reviewer, who may quote brief passages in critical articles or reviews.

ISBN: 979-8-218-46292-5

Cover and book design by Jess LaGreca, Mayfly book design

Library of Congress Catalog Number: 2024913260
First Printing: 2024

Contents

Chapter 1
Childhood 1

Chapter 2
Serving the State 9

Chapter 3
At Sea 15

Chapter 4
The Great Escape 21

Chapter 5
New Possibilities 33

Chapter 6
America 39

Chapter 7
The Waldorf-Astoria 45

Chapter 8
Maturity 63

Chapter 9
A Homecoming 81

Chapter 10
Tropical Beginnings 99

Chapter 11
A Final Lap of Luxury 111

Chapter 12
Coda 123

My Lifelong Journey of Friendship and Special
    Relationships 129

A Passport to Luxury: A World of Opulent Escapes 139

Praise for the Author 142

CHAPTER 1

Childhood

My story begins in the austere aftermath of war in Freiberg, Saxony, where I was born in November 1943 to my parents, Martin and Herta Richter. Before the war, my father was a tailor by trade, but in a desperate bid to avoid conscription, he joined the Party and was sent to the coal mines. There, he also oversaw Russian prisoners of war, sharing his scant food rations and providing them some of our clothes and shoes—a risky act of kindness that could have sent him to the Russian front or executed had he been caught. His compassion during those harsh times earned him the prisoners' respect, which later saved him when, at war's end, the Russian military jailed him. After three months, thanks to the advocacy of those he helped, he was released, unexpectedly arriving at our home in a truck laden with food that was unceremoniously dumped on our street.

Freiberg is just a short journey from the cultural beacon of Dresden. In the waning days of February 1945, Dresden was devastated by firebombing that claimed over 120,000 lives, obliterating the zoo and leaving no refuge, with even the river Elbe aflame. Despite its lack of military significance, Dresden's fate was sealed by becoming part of the Russian-occupied zone of Germany. Following reunification in 1989, Dresden was painstakingly restored, once again sparkling as a jewel, attracting tourists worldwide.

Back in Freiberg, my father continued to work in the mines after a brief period making Russian uniforms—no other tailoring work was available—

until he passed away, of lung cancer contracted at the coal mines, at the age of 65.

In the bleak years after the war, the oppressive communist regime left my family struggling. My father's work in the coal mines during and after the conflict, even with the grueling 10-hour shifts, could not sufficiently provide for us. Recognizing this, my mother, Herta Richter, took a bold step. She leased and revived a small, war-abandoned restaurant, leveraging the permission still granted to East German families to operate small businesses.

The first years of operating our family's restaurant were grueling, and our living accommodations, adjacent to the restaurant itself, were cramped. Before dawn, my siblings and I peeled potatoes with my mother and prepared the restaurant for the day's business. Buying food from a grocer was difficult in those days; families had ration cards that strictly limited how much and what types of food they could legally acquire. And although my parents could access a state-controlled food dispensary for small business owners, they were able to add even more items to their food supply by setting up a small farm in the back of the restaurant, where they raised chicken, geese, and two pigs. It was in that small backyard farm where we picked fresh flowers to arrange in jars on the restaurant tables and checked for new eggs in the chicken coop. A vegetable bed provided the greens, and two apple trees and a pear tree, whose fruits I couldn't wait to shake down after they ripened, provided us with a sweet distraction. After school, we headed straight to the kitchen to wash the dishes and mop the sticky beer puddles that had dried up on the floor.

The local university students were a staple at our family's restaurant, and they walked from their dormitories to mix with the other patrons. A rowdy bunch of both East German and international students, they consumed beer and schnapps as they laughed and joked with each other while playing cards and dice at the dining tables. Despite their sometimes boisterous behavior, my parents treated the students as if they were their own children, always showing them kindness and understanding. If a student couldn't pay their bill, an IOU note was kindly accepted, with the understanding that they would pay it back as soon as they were able. My siblings and I enjoyed watching the interaction between the students and the rest of the customers, and we always looked forward to the lively atmosphere they brought to the restaurant.

At the helm of the entire operation was my mother, Herta Richter. Her success in running our small but enduring family enterprise was not a case of beginner's luck. Before she married my father, my mother served as the housekeeper for an old, retired Saxon prince, who had decamped with his princess to a castle near Berlin in the early 1920s. There, in her black uniform and starched white apron, my mother supervised the castle's maids, cooks, and gardeners. She was extremely organized and meticulous, with a sharp eye for fine details and high quality, traits both demanded from and cultivated by her aristocratic employers.

A heartwarming portrait of my parents, Herta and Martin Richter, the pillars of my strength and ambition.

A nod to my teenage years, clad in traditional lederhosen, in the backyard of our family home in Freiberg, a testament to the times when we grew our own vegetables for the restaurant.

Left: My christening day, gathered with my siblings in Freiberg in early 1944.

Below: A rare gathering of family: my three brothers, my sister, and their respective spouses, each one a staple of our shared history.

From memory to reality—my parents' restaurant as it stood during a nostalgic trip back to Freiberg in 1994.

The beating heart of my hometown—a picturesque shot of the city center of Freiberg.

CHAPTER 2

Serving the State

For three years, beginning at age 14, I woke up at five in the morning, two or three times a week, to board the 6:30 train to Karl-Marx-Stadt (now Chemnitz). Once there, I had to endure the cold walk from the train station to the trade school. This was life as an apprentice in East Germany. The government had allowed my two older brothers to advance to higher education, but it decided that I would be relegated straight to a profession—one of the government's choosing, of course. Until this point, my public education was actually a good one, at least scholastically. We had rigorous studies in all subjects, including mathematics, physics, chemistry, geography, and other languages in addition to German. But there were other subjects we were required to master—specifically communist ones, such as learning Russian, attending Marxist political seminars, and working on the farms. Receiving top marks in those courses was considered a more important accomplishment than being successful in any other subject. But those marks did not matter much now. All the ambition I had for furthering my education was crushed by the stifling political realities of the day. My initial professional desire was to have a profession that combined excitement and status—a translator, an airline steward, something that would take me far away from East Germany. But my family had no clout within the East German Communist Party, and in 1958, after middle school, the government offered me three decidedly less exotic options. I was to choose between farming, construction, and hospitality. The options were limited, but the decision was clear—I would follow in my mother's footsteps. This was how I ended up on the morning train to Karl-Marx-Stadt.

During my hotel and restaurant apprenticeship, my supervisors stifled any seeds of resistance we may have had by exposing us to endless and mind-numbing political propaganda.

If any of the young apprentices expressed disapproval of the Communist Party or its positions, they would be demoted and interrogated. In short, their lives would be made miserable. I worried that my family's lack of political involvement would prevent me from advancing professionally, and I resented the stifling East German communist apparatus. I realized soon enough, however, that I would need to play it smart and adapt to the party's requests—at least publicly. I learned to never express even a hint of anti-communism, even though I came from an anti-communist family. If I wanted to strive for greater heights, I would have to do it on the government's terms. Occasionally, my supervisors would dangle in front of us opportunities to study abroad if we graduated at the top of the apprentice class. One of those opportunities was the chance to participate in an exchange program in Budapest, a cosmopolitan hub at the time. And even though I did graduate at the top, the government moved the goal posts even further out of reach, maintaining that I had fallen short of the ideological expectations of an East German communist representative in Hungary. Maybe because of the relentless rejections and constant pushback, I felt motivated to strive for more, to achieve a fulfilling life with more promising opportunities.

Here and there, the hope of something bigger, of a more interesting world, would appear in wafts and glimmers. In the evenings after our shifts, my fellow apprentices and I would go out to local restaurants and dancing halls in Karl-Marx-Stadt and Freiberg, where the bands played schmaltzy Schlager tunes only our parents thought were modern. But sometimes we got lucky, and the newer and more rousing sounds of American rock 'n' roll (which never exceeded the 20 percent Western entertainment ratio imposed by the government) flowed across the dance hall.

Against the drab backdrop of Karl-Marx-Stadt, the town named after the grandfather of communist ideology, I sang and twisted to Bill Haley & His Comets. And even though some of the older party members threatened to kick me out of the restaurant if I didn't 'tame down' my obviously

Western-inspired dancing, for the time being, it would be my only opportunity to channel some freedom and express myself.

During this time of my life, we had to be very cognizant of what we were saying and doing because of the very real likelihood of being spied upon by the secret police, or *Stasi*, who encouraged and actually demanded that neighbors, friends, and family report any suspicious conversations they overheard. Fortunately, I had a new profession, which my parents encouraged me to pursue wholeheartedly with the hopes that I would one day take over their restaurant. Little did they know, things would turn out very differently for them and for me.

A memento from my humble beginnings, navigating the tough world of hospitality during my apprenticeship in Freiberg.

Above: Choosing my destiny—my hospitality apprenticeship in East Germany, a path I proudly accepted, over construction and farming.

Left: Donned in a tie, an eager student among my classmates, during my school years in Karl-Marx-Stadt.

The MS *Völkerfreundschaft*—a picture of the ship where I landed my first real job post-hospitality apprenticeship, a critical stepping stone in my journey.

CHAPTER 3

At Sea

At 17, I finished my hospitality apprenticeship. Despite graduating at the top of my class, the East German government denied me the opportunity to continue my education at a hotel management school. Complicating things further was the building of the Berlin Wall that summer and the closing of the borders to West Germany, which halted all movement into the western part of Berlin and West Germany.

Before 1961, Berlin was easily accessible to East Germans. In fact, several hundred thousand East Germans crossed into West Berlin between the founding of the GDR in 1949 and the construction of the Berlin Wall in 1961. This new fortress not only tore my country into two separate parts; it also became a physical reminder of my political disadvantage. I despaired at not being born on the "right side" of the Wall's border. Not only was I forbidden from crossing into the western part of Berlin and West Germany after the wall went up, I was also terrified of the minefields and self-shooting machine guns that were installed to ward off trespassers. Amidst this climate of fear, some resorted to a subterranean escape; tunnels were covertly dug beneath the city, connecting East to West. However, these were fraught with danger, frequently discovered by the *Stasi*, and sealed before they could serve as a route to freedom. Being blocked from advancing to hotel management school, I stayed in Freiberg to work lowly jobs at the local hotels. At this time, one could not quit a government job unless transferring to another. In my case, I circumvented this by joining my parents' private restaurant business, a loophole the GDR, eager to draw private employees into government roles, turned a blind eye to. Although I was now a trained, full-fledged waiter, it soon became clear to me that there was no future for me in Freiberg. I needed something new.

That opportunity came in the role as a steward on East Germany's only cruise ship, the MS *Völkerfreundschaft*, which was managed by the state as an *Urlauberschiff*, or holiday ship, for members of the Free German Trade Union Confederation (FDGB) and other paying passengers. Being a steward on the MS *Völkerfreundschaft*, which was previously called the MS *Stockholm* before being purchased by the GDR, came with two significant advantages. First, it literally expanded my horizons and showed me parts of the world I had never seen before. The ship was small, at just 190 meters and 390 passengers, but it was an exemplar of beautiful mid-century craftsmanship, done up in light Swedish wood and furnished with subdued, but elegant, fixtures. I shared a cabin with another steward, and after service hours, we were permitted to congregate in the empty main dining room where, after all the guests retreated back to their cabins or continued on to the ship's other restaurant and bar, we were fed breakfast, lunch, and dinner.

The MS *Völkerfreundschaft* was a ship with a long history of its own that included a famous collision with the SS *Andrea Doria* near New York Harbor in 1956. The SS *Andrea Doria* sank as a result of this collision, and the MS *Völkerfreundschaft* (then still the MS *Stockholm*) lost its foreship. The crew of the MS *Völkerfreundschaft* felt as privileged to be on that ship as the guests we served on the veranda deck and the dining rooms inside. I enjoyed comfortable work accommodations, an opportunity to mingle with important guests, and access to some hard currency with which I could buy Western goods. In those days, you could trade a carton of Marlboro cigarettes from the ship for one kilogram of the finest caviar at many of the Black Sea ports, such as Yalta and Sochi.

More importantly, the job on the MS *Völkerfreundschaft* offered me what was perhaps the most viable escape route from East Germany. At some points on the ship's journeys on the sea, jumping off the deck became a tempting illusion. Occasionally, when our ship would pass through the Mediterranean, and the sun-drenched shores of Sicily, Messina, and Palermo appeared nearly within reach from the deck, we considered leaping right off the railing and swimming to freedom. But the distance between ship and land was far more vast than our eyes led us to believe. I remember one man jumped off the ship near the Sicilian coast, thinking he could quickly swim to land and go unnoticed. He couldn't. And those who tried were immediately picked up by lifeboats, sent back home, and taken to prison.

It was in the Bosporus, on our way to resort destinations in the Black Sea, where the opportunity to jump off the ship was somewhat more feasible. I had seen people attempt to escape during previous arrivals in the Bosporus Strait, a narrow passage that requires the ship to stop and bring on a local and more seasoned pilot to maneuver it through. During that tightrope balancing act of maritime navigation, some people jumped off the ship. But those people usually had family or paid help waiting for them in small boats, where they were quickly hauled to shore. I had no such arrangements and eventually abandoned this fantasy altogether. On later trips, nobody was even allowed to stand on the deck near the railings anymore.

One day, about a year into my job on the ship, it was announced that we would journey across the Atlantic to visit Havana and Santiago de Cuba. With one month at sea, our voyage to communist Cuba would be our longest and most demanding journey yet. At first, leaving the port at Warnemünde, East Germany, that autumn of 1962 felt as commonplace as all our other journeys. But eventually, it became clear that we would see only a vast blue expanse for an entire month, except for the Azores, which broke up the monotony roughly halfway through our journey. The oceanic expanse was beginning to take its disorienting toll until one day, quite literally out of the blue, the island of Cuba emerged on the horizon. At first, I thought my eyes were playing tricks on me after a couple of weeks at sea, but as we got closer, I could see this was no mirage. Interrupting this oceanic reverie was an American destroyer that cut off access to Havana, and checked every ship to see if it violated the blockade President John F. Kennedy had recently imposed on Cuba. The MS *Völkerfreundschaft* was the first ship to attempt passing through the blockade, and we were approached by a destroyer and an airplane flying uncomfortably low overhead and taking pictures of the ships below. When they saw we were not a commercial or military ship carrying missiles, they let us pass. All the other ships were sent back. As it turns out, our arrival in Cuba coincided directly with the strained negotiations of the Cuban Missile Crisis, which was as close as the U.S. had ever gotten to nuclear war, and suddenly we were unwitting spectators to a dramatic Cold War scene. I remember seeing, as we arrived in Havana, the giant wrought-iron sign over the harbor entrance that welcomed seafarers to Cuba: *Patria o Muerte*, fatherland or death.

Cuba was unlike anything I had ever seen before. It was exotic, tropical, warm, and sensuous. That night, after our ship finally made it to the harbor, some crewmates and I decided to disembark and roam a world previously available to us only in dreams. Palm trees swayed in the tropical breeze, and wafts of spicy rum and cigar perfumed the humid air. As dusk turned to night, the streets began teeming with energy, and the bars filled up with beautiful women and military men. A friend and I walked into one of the bars, which on the newly Communist island still sold some western products, hoping for a Coca-Cola or something similarly foreign to us. Because I spoke neither Spanish nor English, my friendly greeting of "How old are you?" to one of the young girls at the bar was misunderstood by her and her friend as "How much do you charge?" So, while Kennedy was negotiating with Khrushchev, it turns out that my friend and I were unwittingly negotiating with the ladies of the night. Realizing that we had a curfew, and that the girls were less interested in us and more interested in our ability to pay in dollars, which we did not have, we headed back to the ship without consummating our desired transactions. The next morning, we woke up with a shock: The ship would be turning around immediately, taking some of the island's East German diplomats back with us, and heading back to East Germany. Apparently, while we were gallivanting in the streets of Havana, the U.S. had threatened to bomb Havana in retaliation for a successful Cuban attempt to shoot down an American plane. Cuba was no longer a safe destination for our ship or crew. We never did make it to Santiago de Cuba, and with that, the whims of our international leaders had cut short our Cuban journey.

Fresh-faced and brimming with anticipation, my shipmates and I dress in our lifejackets, ready to embark on our new jobs aboard the MS *Völkerfreundschaft*.

Promotional material from the MS *Völkerfreundschaft*, highlighting amenities for members of the FDGB, an East German labor union.

CHAPTER 4

The Great Escape

After returning from our short trip to Cuba, normal business resumed. However, it would be another year before the MS *Völkerfreundschaft* embarked on another dramatic journey. The ship's captain announced that the ship would carry a congress of medical doctors on its first journey to Western Europe since the construction of the Berlin Wall. Because of the supposed risks involved, the crew would be selected from an exclusive group of mostly married men and women, who were thought to be less likely to escape, given that one of their spouses would remain back home. Despite being single, I was granted an exception and given the privilege of joining the journey because I had recently been recognized as the ship's Employee of the Year. Two weeks before we embarked, I was permitted to make a short trip home. I had told my supervisors that I wanted to go to Freiberg for my cousin's christening, but that was a lie. I needed a good excuse to return and say goodbye, in case I never saw Freiberg again.

From the port in Warnemünde, I traveled five hours southbound by rail to visit my home. The train was overcrowded with people returning to the cities after their summer vacations on the Baltic Sea. Next to me, in the packed train car, sat an American student who was a few years older than me. He didn't speak German, and I didn't speak English, but we nevertheless attempted to acquaint ourselves by agreeing to speak in our broken French.

Perhaps it was because this American stranger exhibited no viable threat, or maybe because the vast language gap between us gave me a false sense of security, but an impulse overtook me and I let slip to him that I was planning to escape East Germany, once and for all, when the MS *Völkerfreundschaft* set sail for Western Europe later that month. Maybe my slip of the tongue was really just a subconscious confession, a need to expel the anxiety brewing in my chest, but putting my plans into actual words made my decision feel real and tangible.

There was no turning back now. My new American friend, an art history student at Columbia University, stared at me for a second, shrugged, and laughed me off, shaking his head in disbelief. He was friendly but oblivious to my distress. I wasn't sure how seriously he took my scheme. Nevertheless, he gave me his phone number when we disembarked in Dresden, and I promised to one day be in touch again.

When I arrived at our family's home in Freiberg, I gave one of my brothers a box of my most important items—including my favorite clothes, books, and watches—and chose to reveal my plans only to him. The rest of my family would learn of my escape, successful or not, only after I had attempted it. After three restful days at home, it was time to return back north to the ship. I hugged my mother and sister goodbye, trying to act casually but knowing deep down it would be a long time before I saw them or Freiberg again. As I left the house, my mother turned to my sister and said to her, without hesitation, "I don't think he's coming back."

I returned to the port in Warnemünde on the Baltic Sea and boarded the MS *Völkerfreundschaft* for what I hoped would be the final time. We then set sail on a journey to the Black Sea, making our first stop in Gdansk, Poland, followed by Leningrad, and then Helsinki. At that time, Finland was a neutral nation, but due to its close proximity to the Soviet Union, it was not the safest point of escape. The country was infested with Soviet sympathizers and spies, and I figured it would be wiser to wait one more stop before I attempted any sort of escape in earnest. This would end up being a good decision: In our subsequent stop in Stockholm, a select number of crew members were permitted to disembark and sightsee the city in groups of four. Although I was expected back on board that afternoon to prepare service for the physicians' banquet, I would also be allowed to sightsee. I tagged along with three crewmates who happened to be off-duty that day. They would not be expected to return to the ship in a timely manner, and so they were less likely to notice my own scheme unfold. I took an umbrella and, wearing extra clothes underneath my outfit, grabbed my coat, even though it was the dead of summer. I was terrified of raising suspicion—but at least I had some clothes on my back to last me for a few days. I shuffled down the cobblestone streets of Stockholm with my fellow crew members, sweaty and uncomfortable in all my extra garments, hoping to distract my friends by guiding them deeper into the city and farther away from the port. By mid-afternoon we were in the heart of Stockholm, far enough from the MS *Völkerfreundschaft*. At that point, I announced to my shipmates, who were in no rush to return to the ship, that I needed to head back immediately for the reception that evening. I would take a taxi, I said, and they would stay behind, not rush, and enjoy themselves. I left them for a more discreet street corner where I could safely hail a taxi. Little did they know, I would not be returning to port.

When I finally summoned a taxicab, I found myself saying, almost automatically, "To the West German Embassy, please." I had learned to say that in English and had practiced it at home in anticipation of this moment. I was surprised by how shaky my voice sounded.

The taxi driver glanced up and made eye contact with me through his rear-view mirror. Did he know? My god, I thought, Now I was *really* trapped. Did he wish to turn me in? The consequences of that action would be unforgiving but not surprising. You see, we were raised to expect constant espionage, to assume that all of our actions were being closely monitored by people we thought were friends. The Ministry for State Security in East Germany, or the *Stasi*, recruited thousands of everyday, ordinary citizens to serve as spies for the GDR, both domestically and abroad. Everybody knew somebody back home who was informing the *Stasi* of their neighbors' actions. It was not unlikely for this random taxicab driver to be looking for young men like myself to turn for defection, or *Republikflucht*.

But the driver simply glanced back down at his wheel, put the car in gear and drove me to the embassy, just as I'd requested. Relief flooded through me. I gave him the only 20 Swedish Crowns I possessed, not knowing if it was enough or too much, and scurried out of his car as quickly as I could upon arrival. I walked to the embassy door and told the security guard the truth: I was seeking political asylum. The guards at the West German Embassy in Stockholm were initially skeptical of my request, but once they saw that I was serious, standing there with my few belongings, I was ushered in and escorted to a secure office, to be processed and given a temporary passport to West Germany. I knew that West Germany was committed, at least on paper, to supporting refugees from the GDR and other Warsaw Pact countries with asylum. But I did not know of anybody who had done it successfully. All I knew at the time was this: Since the construction of the Berlin Wall, fewer than 20,000 people had successfully escaped the GDR. Escaping East Germany after 1961 was a gamble that called for "unusual imagination and resourcefulness," according to a New York Times article published that year. I don't know if I possessed either of those traits in great quantity, but I knew that against all odds, I had finally made it.

That evening, the officers at the West German Embassy in Stockholm placed me on a guarded train, which took me to the Refugee Receiving Center in Giessen, West Germany, because I had no friends or relatives to take me in. The refugee center was where asylum seekers—Hungarians, Czechs, East Germans—arrived to be processed and filtered by authorities if they did not have relatives to house them. When I arrived at Giessen after the 16-hour journey, it was midnight on Saturday, raining and cold. I was given soap, toothpaste, a toothbrush, two pillows, and a blanket. I had a basic, no-frills room, which I shared with a Hungarian refugee. The following Monday, CIA agents and West German secret service agents started to interrogate me. Both gentlemen were very courteous, and their line of questioning seemed innocuous enough—they even paid me for my time. It was explained to me that thorough interrogation was a necessity, given the massive influx of spies from the East who had infiltrated West Germany by the thousands. Since my escape from the ship was relatively unchallenging, they needed to confirm that I wasn't one of these spies. Perhaps there was even the consideration of recruiting me to their ranks, given the scrutiny of their questions. They probed me directly about the layouts of Russian harbors and requested sketches of certain areas, inquired about the military presence, uniforms, and types of weapons. Although I suspected they were already well-informed on these matters, my responses could serve to demonstrate my potential "talents" to them. But when the interrogation wound down and I was cleared to leave, the administrators asked me where I wanted to go now. I found myself at a loss for words. Where did I want to go now? I had nowhere to go. Nothing to do. I finally said that I wished to work on another cruise ship in West Germany. Being on a ship felt like home to me—it came with a uniform and a purpose. It was a profession I knew how to perform. The authorities helped me to get settled: They supplied me with a new set of clothes, a pocket sum of starter money, and a West German passport. Then they put me on a train from Giessen to Bremerhaven, a harbor on the Baltic Sea, to sign up for work on the MS *Berlin* and live in a nearby labor camp. I was 21 years old, alone, and homesick.

After this second long journey, unable to find my way to the camp from the train station, I stopped in front of the home of an elderly couple and asked them for directions. They looked at me curiously and asked if I was one of the newly arrived refugees they had read about in the newspaper. I told them that yes, I was, and they directed me to the camp.

The next day, the supervisor in charge of the camp approached me and said that Dorothy and Claus Mazura, the couple who had given me directions to the camp, had phoned to invite me over for dinner the following night. What started as a single dinner eventually became a comforting routine for me. Dorothy and Claus became my surrogate family, and they opened their home to me for many years while I served on the MS *Berlin* and TS *Bremen*, another West German cruise ship. So in between voyages, I would return to my adoptive home, grateful to have this generous couple caring for me while my real parents remained separated by cement barriers and divisive ideologies.

During one of our trips, which took us through numerous Caribbean islands, we made a stop in Curaçao, known not just for its idyllic beaches but also as a major Shell Oil harbor for oil tankers. Curaçao accommodated the many sailors' needs and desires with the largest bordello known as Gambralego. It was quite a sight, observing sailors from these tankers pile into buses destined for an evening at Gambralego, in pursuit of leisure and distraction from their sea-bound duties.

My duties as a steward on the MS *Berlin* and TS *Bremen* were similar to the ones I performed on the MS *Völkerfreundschaft*. Although I had to reestablish myself from square one on a West German cruise ship, I was grateful to be working on any ship at all. Most exciting of all, though, was the ship's upcoming journey to New York. It was not my first time crossing the Atlantic— you will recall my short-lived voyage to Cuba—but it would be my first time going to the United States. The Statue of Liberty greeted us on the way to the New York Harbor, and upon disembarking, in the autumn of 1964, I headed uptown to see the greatest hotel in the world: The Waldorf-Astoria. At that time, The Waldorf-Astoria was the unofficial palace of the world.

Even I, a recently graduated hospitality professional from Freiberg, knew that. From the outside, I took in the formidable black and green marble façade of the hotel and the gilded flourishes. The building, which occupied an entire city block, simultaneously expressed a sense of old-world luxury and modernist severity. It was the epitome of luxury. Little did I know that in about a decade, I would get to know it intimately from the inside as well. From a nearby payphone on Madison Avenue, I called the student from Columbia University whom I met on the train before my escape, the same one to whom I had confessed my grand plans.

He answered the phone and, in broken French, our only shared language, I told him *Je l'ai fait!* I had made it.

An enduring symbol of camaraderie: flanked by my shipmates after my escape to West Germany, while working on the MS *Berlin* and TS *Bremen*.

A token from the past—a postcard of the
MS *Berlin*, the ship that became my workplace
after my daring escape from East Germany.

A piece of history—a postcard featuring the TS *Bremen*, another ship that became a professional haven post-escape.

A frame from my formative years—in the bustling kitchen of Hotel Touring and Red Ox in Basel, where I honed my skills before my studies in Heidelberg.

CHAPTER 5

New Possibilities

Work on the MS *Berlin* was difficult, but the rhythms of my week felt much too similar to the ones I had just left behind. After all, I didn't escape my life in East Germany to do the same things on the other side of the border, particularly because life on board was filled with hardships. In Claus and Dorothy's kitchen, I scoured the newspaper's classified sections for job openings and eventually found a busboy position in Basel, Switzerland, at the charming Hotel Touring and Red Ox. At the time, Switzerland was the epitome of *hôtellerie* and was looked upon as the most sophisticated center for fine hospitality training. Although I was not eager to start my career as a busboy again, I knew I would be getting my foot in the door to the mecca of the hospitality profession. Those first years in Switzerland were my real professional coming of age. In four short years, I had advanced from *commis de rang*, to *demi chef*, to *chef de rang*, to *chef de service*, and finally, to director of restaurants. I was finally finding myself in the West. In front of me, I had access to an entire world of professional possibilities, which was something I could only dream of in the suffocating confines of East Germany. I worked hard during those years to deepen my experience in the hotel industry. It wasn't all studies and work, though.

One day I took my girlfriend's Volkswagen and drove, on a whim, and without having made reservations, to the French Riviera for a week. The drive from Basel to Nice was at least eight hours, but the promise of the open road along the coasts and landscapes, and the chance to experience the luxury of the Riviera, was much too tempting. As I arrived, the azure blue shoreline of Nice and the enclaves of the rich and famous unfolded before me. I eventually arrived at a boutique hotel I felt would suit me appropriately for my short vacation. Little did I know, the hotel I had randomly stumbled upon was the Hôtel du Cap-Eden-Roc, Cap d'Antibes, which at that time was the most exclusive and luxurious hotel on the French Riviera. Although I arrived late and the rate afforded me a closet-sized room for only one night, I would make the most out of it. The next morning, like an impostor among the wealthy, I basked outside near the swimming pool, which was carved out of imposing rock, and enjoyed a leisurely breakfast on the hotel's perfumed terraces. Unable to afford to continue my stay, I checked out of the Eden-Roc the following morning and drove a few miles west toward Cannes, stopping at Juan Les Pins. The Ambassador Hotel, a more affordable accommodation, would be my home for four nights.

On my first night at the Ambassador, I went down to the dining room and was seated near a young, handsome couple. The lady was very friendly and beautiful, but her boyfriend had a different kind of charm altogether. The man was Hubert Krantz who, I would soon learn, was the heir of a major industrial family in Aachen, Germany. On the surface, Hubert was a typically rich young man, handsome and self-confident, a man who cruised the French Riviera with one model girlfriend after another, summer after summer. But he was not just some run-of-the-mill playboy. Hubert was one of the most generous men I would ever come to know.

Hubert lived in Cologne, and I admired not just his business success but his genuine curiosity for life. Hubert studied precious gems, wellness, and nutrition. He also held a doctorate in economics from St. Gallen University in Switzerland and independently consulted for firms across the world. Not long after Hubert and I became friendly, I confided in him my desire to choose a career in hospitality. Why I was expecting scorn or judgment from Hubert, I couldn't say for sure. Maybe I felt self-conscious in front of an industry titan, a capitalist striver. But Hubert's eyes lit up when I told him my plans, and he encouraged me to apply to a hotel management school in Heidelberg. At the time, Heidelberg had one of the finest hotel management schools, not only in Germany but in all of Europe. I could forego school altogether and keep floating around the world, he said, but I would never truly reach the professional heights I was dreaming of without a degree. Hubert and I remained close friends for many years until his personal circumstances changed. His investments had gone sour, the consulting firm he opened began to flounder, and his untempered generosity had gotten him into a financial abyss he was not able to confront. After many years, he succumbed to suicide. Despite his many girlfriends, perhaps no woman took Hubert's death harder than his longtime secretary, an older single woman who, upon hearing of his suicide, placed her head in the oven and turned on the gas.

The force of Hubert's charisma and his skills of persuasion gave me the push I needed to apply to the hotel management school in Heidelberg, one of the most charming cities in Germany. Heidelberg is a small but energetic college town with a stunning medieval castle overlooking the view from a hilltop. The truth is, I did not have the qualifications to attend the hotel management school there. I did not even have a high school diploma. But the university made an exception because of my professional experience and refugee status. I would need to keep up with all the students who already had degrees and prove myself, academically, to the faculty. At night, I crammed extra economics courses and caught up to the rest of the students, who had been accepted primarily on their academic merits. Fortunately, I had four great friends who tutored me along the way. Together, we spent hours over textbooks and lecture notes, and their guidance was crucial in helping me bridge the educational gap.

One area in which I held an advantage over my classmates in Heidelberg was my restaurant experience, and I supplemented my knowledge by taking a four-month specialized course in restaurant management. I received a certificate, or *Meisterbrief*, that allowed me to teach apprentices and students at the university as an assistant teacher, lecturing on the art of service, tableside cooking, and restaurant management. It not only gave me a paycheck but it built my confidence. Here I was, an East German boy who grew up helping his mother prepare food in her small restaurant, now lecturing to a room full of selected students who were lacking in this part of their practical education. I was finally able to see the future ahead of me.

Heidelberg, however, was not just a place of rigorous academics and relentless studying; it was also where I forged some lifelong friendships that have withstood the test of time. One such relationship began with Peter Messerschmitt, a fellow classmate who shared my journey from our school days in Heidelberg, starting in 1969. As we navigated the challenges of the hotel management program, Peter and I found some cheer in each other's company, often escaping the pressures of our studies to share friendly moments off campus. Our friendship endured long after our time in Heidelberg, and we remained in close contact, supporting each other through our respective career trajectories. As life unfolded, I had the pleasure of meeting and becoming close to Peter's partner, Angelica, and his children. Together, they became an integral part of my life, and we shared not just our professional interests but also our personal milestones and celebrations.

After graduating as a *Betriebswirt*, or a business graduate, in hotel economics, I was awarded a one-year scholarship from the Washington Hilton in Washington, D.C., for a general management training program with additional studies at Cornell University in Ithaca, New York. This scholarship was a great honor that was offered to me by Dieter Huckestein, then the Director of Food and Beverage at the Washington Hilton, who was himself a German and a graduate of Heidelberg. Huckestein later became the president of Hilton Hotels for several years.

Initially, I was selected to receive the scholarship for a different hotel, but a classmate contested the outcome, claiming that he had a slightly higher grade point average than mine. Huckestein took note of this and decided to create a second scholarship. He offered it to me, and I accepted it eagerly.

Left: Everlasting bonds: My dear friend Peter Messerschmitt and his longtime partner Angelica, pillars of friendship.

Below: Marianne Willareth, my cherished friend from Basel, Switzerland, who recently turned 100 years old. Our bond sparked in 1966 and deepened over years, our conversations a daily comfort.

Caught in a moment of levity with Hubert Kranz at my home in the Hamptons in the 1990s. A dear friend from Cologne, his friendship was a beacon through the decades.

CHAPTER 6

America

I arrived in Washington, D.C., in May of 1972, with three hundred dollars in my pocket and very little English in my vocabulary. Americans then were enjoying relative economic prosperity and had grown somewhat numb to the carnage thousands of miles away in Vietnam. That fall, President Richard Nixon would be reelected in a landslide. It was against this political backdrop that I began my first American hotel internship at one of the city's busiest hotels: the Washington Hilton. In the early 1970s, the hotel was a prime destination for top diplomats, cabinet officials, international delegations, Capitol Hill staffers, and lobbyists who represented every conceivable industry.

During this time, the late King Hussein of Jordan was one of the royal dignitaries who visited Washington, D.C. It was a very impressive encounter considering he was the first king I had ever come into contact with. He dined, of course, in his suite, and I was put in charge of his room service needs. To my surprise, he addressed me in French and seemed pleased that I could converse with him in his preferred language.

Shortly thereafter, Sammy Davis Jr.—a legend in his own right and a king of entertainment—swung by with his entourage. Once more, I was on room service duty. He was all charisma, and on his departure, he gave me a hearty handshake and announced to those present that I was his "only white brother." His playful endorsement brought a chuckle to everyone around and left me with a sense of having made it—not just on the job, but on a level of personal connection that transcended barriers, a true "rat pack" moment for the books.

My roommate in the program was a young man by the name of Bill Edwards III, who started his internship at the Washington Hilton on the same day as I did. We were paired by the program as a sort of exercise in cultural exchange: Bill would absorb some of my "old-world hospitality" training, and I would become appropriately "Americanized." The exchange was, for the most part, equal except for one very large difference: My father had worked in a coal mine, and Bill's father was the president of Hilton Hotels.

Over time, Bill and I exchanged stories, and he and his wife Patty eventually would become my good friends. One of our favorite memories was of the Capitol City Republican Club's breakfast banquet for the newly-inaugurated President Nixon. More than 2,000 guests and dignitaries were invited to the inaugural breakfast at the Washington Hilton's large ballroom, including the mayor of Moscow, Vladimir Promyslov. Prior to the main event, President Nixon gave a short speech in a private room to a more intimate gathering of international dignitaries, including Mayor Promyslov. The problem? Mr. Promyslov did not speak English, and his interpreter was nowhere to be found!

Back in the service area, unaware of the havoc outside, I was busy preparing for the breakfast service when suddenly my supervisor came rushing in to find me. I was to come into the ballroom immediately, he announced. As I hurriedly made my way to the ballroom, my mind raced with the possibilities of what I could have done wrong in the kitchen. Imagine my surprise when I was informed that I was needed to translate President Nixon's speech for the mayor of Moscow, whose interpreter had not yet arrived. At that moment I realized that my supervisors and the event organizers had remembered my East German roots—in East Germany, Russian was routinely taught in schools. Though my Russian was far from fluent, it was still more advanced than my English, which at the time was still quite poor. It was with a mix of gratitude and anxiety that I accepted the task, praying that I would not disappoint the Moscow mayor or President Nixon with my faulty translation. But thankfully, just before I could start, the interpreter arrived in a rush, and I was able to return to the kitchen with a sigh of relief.

As time went on, my friendship with Bill Edwards and his brother Bradley grew even stronger. Bradley was a student at Georgetown University, but during the summers he worked for me as a busboy. The Edwards family liked me so much that they invited me to their gatherings in Beverly Hills. I even became the godfather to Bradley's son, Brendan. My ability to build relationships and form close connections with people who could help me succeed once again paid off. However, there were downsides to this as well. My colleagues were envious of my connections with one of the most powerful hospitality families in the United States. To prove myself, I had to work even harder and perform twice as well so I could dispel any notions that I was receiving special treatment. Despite the challenges, I knew that my dedication and hard work would ultimately speak for itself.

While my adventures were continuing, East Germany was celebrating the 25th anniversary of its communist government, and as part of the 'magnanimity' of those celebrations, the GDR was offering amnesty to all former East German refugees who had escaped the country before 1970. Those refugees would be allowed to visit their homeland, but if it had been up to the GDR, the refugees would have been forced to stay there forever. I was one of those refugees. But I was skeptical. Would I be arrested upon arrival? Would I be able to return to the United States after my visit? I decided to take the chance anyway and visit my homeland, almost 10 years after I escaped from it.

I flew from New York City's JFK International Airport to Frankfurt and, upon landing at the airport, I visited my adoptive aunt and uncle. Two days later, I got on the eastbound train. As the train got closer to the border, I suddenly became terribly nervous and concerned. The barbed wires, the East German military and police, their German shepherds—all of the terrifying images of my childhood suddenly made me afraid that I had made the wrong decision. Eventually we arrived, and my family came to pick me up from the train station. A wave of relief went through me. I was finally home. I enjoyed six wonderful days with my family. We reflected on old times, and I regaled them with stories from my voyages and my new life. Even so, I was always worried about being picked up and arrested at any time by a KGB agent or the *Stasi*. (Vladmir Putin would eventually be a leading KGB agent in Dresden). Before I knew it, it was time to return. My career in the United States was waiting for me.

My first and only Hilton Hotels stock, a cherished gift from my dear friend Bradley Edwards, whose father was president of Hilton Hotels.

The Waldorf-Astoria, an iconic symbol of opulence and grandeur, captured in its early 20th-century splendor.

CHAPTER 7

The Waldorf-Astoria

After my homecoming visit to East Germany, I returned straight to Chicago, where the president of Hilton Hotels had asked me to work in catering sales at the Palmer House Hotel, a historic hotel first built in 1871 in Chicago's downtown Loop area. Although I was honored to serve at the hotel, the work was a challenge for me. I was used to working as an Assistant Director of Food and Beverage, but Mr. Edwards claimed I needed sales experience under my belt before I could be promoted to the director level. As the long and dreary winter in Chicago wore on, I found myself yearning, once again, for a change of scenery. I had always felt at home on the East Coast, with its rich history and vibrant culture, and I longed to experience it for myself again. As luck would have it, my fortunes took a turn for the better. I was offered a promotion to become the Director of Food and Beverage at the prestigious Rye Town Hilton in Rye Brook, New York. The hotel was one of the finest Hiltons built at the time, and I was eager to take on the new challenge. That said, as much as I enjoyed my job at the Rye Town Hilton, my heart still yearned for the excitement and energy of the big city. That's why, nine months into my new job in Rye Brook, I was elated when I received a call from Frank Wangeman to meet him at his offices at The Waldorf-Astoria.

Frank Wangeman was a German-born hospitality executive who brought his old-world sensibilities to the American world of corporate *hôtellerie*. Born in Frankfurt in 1912, Wangeman, like me, was raised in a hospitality-oriented family—his father managed the legendary Frankfurter Hof hotel for years when Wangeman was young. He eventually trained at the École hôtelière de Lausanne in Lausanne, Switzerland, before moving to the United States in the 1930s to become an assistant manager at The Waldorf-Astoria. Wangeman's eye for detail and the meticulous care he bestowed on his guests at the Waldorf came to the attention of Conrad Hilton, who was a regular guest of the hotel before he purchased it in 1949. Eventually, Wangeman became a close associate of the Hilton tycoon and was hired to manage his most difficult and demanding properties on the East Coast. Wangeman, who was General Manager and Executive Vice President of The Waldorf-Astoria and Senior Vice President of the East Coast for Hilton Hotels, also had a long personal relationship with the Hiltons and enjoyed a privileged seat on the company's board. In other words, when Mr. Wangeman called, you listened.

It would have undoubtedly been the most challenging chapter of my career, but on that call, Wangeman provided me the comforts and trappings in line with such a demanding job, which included a small apartment in the Waldorf Towers. Of course, Wangeman was a shrewd recruiter, and the more challenging realities of living in the hotel soon became apparent. My apartment on the 36th floor was originally designed as servant quarters, where private staff for the hotel's most exclusive guests would sleep. My tiny living room furniture made it look like a dollhouse, and I could reach the window of my bedroom from the bed.

You could not have rented this kind of room to a guest back then, much less today. To make matters more stressful, Wangeman, with his relentless scrutiny, lived just five floors above me, in an enviable suite that overlooked Park Avenue. Living in the hotel, just a short elevator ride away from the Wangeman suite, meant that another manager and I were on-call no fewer than 24 hours almost every day. In those early months on the job, the farthest I could go to escape the pressure on me was just a few blocks, taking an occasional brisk stroll around 49th and 50th Streets. I always knew that Wangeman could call me back to work at any point.

One day, as I settled into my office at The Waldorf-Astoria, I was met with an unusual sight. Laid out before me on my desk, wrapped in a humble sheet of toilet paper, was one of our hotel's prized croissants, accompanied by a note. Scrawled in bold, black ink, it read, "This is a piece of S-H-I-T." The signature at the bottom belonged to none other than Mr. Wangeman. I knew Wangeman had a reputation for being a perfectionist, and I couldn't help but feel a twinge of apprehension as I read the note. His decision not to involve the Executive Chef, a move characteristic of his direct and unorthodox methods, was a clear indication of his expectations—I was to be held accountable for every aspect of the food and beverage operations, down to the finest detail. I knew that I had to rise to the occasion and prove that the croissant in question was worthy of the Waldorf's reputation. Wangeman ordered me to take the Waldorf's limousine and travel to the finest bakeries in the city, so I could compare and evaluate the competition. When I returned to the hotel, I presented Wangeman with three options, each one carefully chosen and evaluated. I asked him if he would like to conduct a blind tasting to determine which one he thought was the superior croissant. After some consideration, he picked one, declaring it to be the best. I gently broke the news to him that the croissant he had selected was, in fact, one of the Waldorf's own. He nodded, but he wouldn't admit defeat. I knew that puncturing his ego too much would not be wise. Still, I couldn't help feeling a sense of satisfaction, knowing that our croissant had stood up to the test and had been deemed the best by Wangeman, the hotel's very own master.

Another time, Wangeman's wife, who was a real lady, sent the staff a list of groceries and pantry items to be ordered and delivered to their suite. We rushed around to get the groceries prepared for the Wangemans. Then we sent all of the items, exquisitely packaged, up to their apartment in the hotel. Several minutes after the food was delivered, I received a call directly from Mr. Wangeman himself, demanding that I come up to the suite immediately! When I arrived, all of the groceries were laid out neatly on the kitchen table. That is, all except for a jar of pickles Mr. Wangeman was holding out in front of his face, which was chiseled into a deep frown. "Try one," Frank Wangeman taunted me. I declined. "Try one!" Wangeman yelled. I stared down at the open jar of pickles that Wangeman had thrust in front of me, and then I looked back up at his face. He glared at me. "They are not crunchy enough!"

In truth, Wangeman had good reason to keep me on my toes: The food and beverage operation at the Waldorf was enormous and required my undivided attention. We had 14 facilities overall, including eight restaurants, several banquet halls, and the best-known night club in New York City, the Empire Room, where on any given night, guests could enjoy performances from Maurice Chevalier, Gladys Knight & The Pips, Chita Rivera, and Peggy

Lee, to name a few. If money was no object—and for many of our guests it wasn't—the Empire Room could become your very own fantasy land for a private event or gathering.

Leona Helmsley, the city's most cut-throat real estate tycoon, held a birthday party there for her husband Harry, in part to shower her devoted husband with an unrivaled show of appreciation, and also to not-so-subtly signal to her guests and competitors that she still reigned as the queen of New York real estate. If there was ever a venue to display one's social dominance, it was The Waldorf-Astoria. Sir Harry's Bar, an elegant, club-like cocktail bar with deep wood panels and checkerboard motifs, was where the city's tourists and powerful men rendezvoused with the ladies of the night, a commodity of which there was no shortage in 1970s New York City. The main restaurants of the hotel included The Peacock Alley, named for the hallway that connected the two original Waldorf towers, the Bull and Bear Steakhouse, home of the high-roller's power lunch, and Oscar's Brasserie, named after Oscar Tschirky, the famous *maître d'hôtel* of The Waldorf-Astoria until his retirement in 1943. We also featured Shah Abbas, a decadent Iranian restaurant where beluga caviar was served by the kilo, and Inagiku, the Japanese restaurant built specially to accommodate the visit of Emperor Hirohito and his extensive entourage. Of course, room service was under my purview as well. And room service in a hotel of more than 1,400 rooms, many of which were occupied by the world's most demanding guests, was a mammoth operation in and of itself. Finally, there were the banquet rooms, which included many meeting rooms and the famous Starlight Room, a large ballroom that could accommodate up to 2,000 guests at a time. The banquet arm of the hotel was legendary in the star power it was able to attract: political fundraisers, black-tie galas, and welcome soirees for international royalty were our norm. In the 1970s, the banquet business alone generated up to $65 million in revenues for the hotel.

Originally, I was not in charge of certain parts of the banquet department. But Wangeman changed that. A large component of the Waldorf's banquet operations included a made-to-order kosher catering to serve our large population of affluent Jewish guests.

Because the Waldorf did not have an in-house kosher kitchen, the director of catering was charged with hiring someone from the city's web of kosher caterers. The caterer would arrive with their specialized staff and, after the kitchen had been made kosher, he would prepare everything right then and there. I was always called in to make sure the fees were properly distributed between the caterer and the hotel, and that every dollar was correctly accounted for.

The politics of the position were not limited to pleasing Mr. Frank Wangeman or the local socialites. The year I started at the Waldorf, Palestinian leader Farouk Khadoumi arrived in New York's JFK International Airport and was transported by a 20-vehicle motorcade, decked out with sharpshooters, to The Waldorf-Astoria. Most of the hotel staff was not made aware of Khadoumi's visit until the moment he stepped out of his limousine, accompanied by an entire armed entourage, and walked into the tower lobby of the hotel where, unbeknownst to us, he had rented 15 suites for his entire posse. The following year, Yasser Arafat, at the time Khadoumi's boss, stayed at the Waldorf under equally controversial circumstances that involved hotel reservations that were secretly made by the U.S. Department of State.

Khadoumi and Arafat may have had politically productive trips to the U.S., but the combination of those visits was destructive to our relationship with the Jewish business community in New York. Upon hearing that Arafat was staying at the Waldorf, much of the Jewish community boycotted the hotel, which culminated in some very turbulent rioting inside and outside the property. Matters got so out of hand that the NYPD, mounted on horses, took security measures to barricade the hotel entrances for protection. This rift with our Jewish business partners and guests was not going to simply resolve itself. We would have to get creative. Fortunately, the opportunity came several months later, when Israeli Prime Minister Golda Meir announced her own plans to visit the United States. With the help of our deep network of kosher caterers and Jewish allies, the hotel was able to convince Meir's staff to accommodate her at The Waldorf-Astoria. With that small act of diplomacy, we mitigated the initial outrage that festered after Arafat's visit, and we mended our relationship with the Jewish community.

In the luxury hotel business, security measures and surveillance systems are paramount, especially considering the high-profile nature of our guests. These protective steps are not merely a matter of guest comfort, but also of safety and reputation. The allure of The Waldorf-Astoria often attracted the attention of unsavory characters—thieves, criminals, and prostitutes. It was not uncommon for prostitutes to frequent the bars, luring unaccompanied guests with their flirtations. These interactions sometimes led to the guests' rooms where, in a number of cases, the individuals found themselves victims of drugging and theft, stripped of wallets, valuables, and jewelry while they were incapacitated.

The morning after, as these men awoke to the harsh reality of their situation, the hotel was often confronted with accusations and demands for compensation. It was in these delicate situations that our security footage proved indispensable. By presenting the evidence to the victims, we recommended filing a police report, which usually deterred them from pursuing any further claims against the hotel—especially the married clientele who wished to avoid the ensuing scandal and public embarrassment.

During my tenure at The Waldorf-Astoria, which also housed the mission of the United States to the United Nations on its top floor, I served Israeli Prime Ministers Golda Meir and Yitzhak Rabin, and most of Europe's royalty, including Queen Elizabeth II, King Carl XVI Gustaf of Sweden, King Carlos and Queen Sofia of Spain, King Olav V of Norway, Queen Juliana of the Netherlands, and Queen Margrethe II of Denmark. Many of these dignitaries came to the U.S. and stayed at the Waldorf to witness and take part in America's Bicentennial celebrations in 1976. The Bicentennial celebrations and the accompanying VIP guests were a professional highlight, and they demanded my utmost thoroughness and perfection. One of our most important guests that year was Japanese Emperor Hirohito, who arrived in New York during the Bicentennial as a final gesture of reconciliation between the United States and Japan.

As the esteemed guests of The Waldorf-Astoria gathered in the grand ballroom for the special event honoring the Emperor, it became immediately clear that this was no ordinary occasion. For one, the 800 members of the Japan Society had assembled in the ballroom with no tables set for lunch because the Emperor and Empress, in accordance with their protocol, did not eat in public. As the Emperor and Empress made their way through the ballroom, walking on the plush red carpet that none of the guests dared to step on, the hotel fell into a hushed silence. Not even a dropped pin could be heard. It was a rare and unforgettable moment, made all the more special by the fact that we were able to play a role in the Emperor's visit and the important gesture of goodwill between the United States and Japan. And though the guests were left to wait for their lunch until the Emperor concluded his speech and returned with the Empress to the Presidential

Suite—an exit accompanied by 800 deeply bowed heads—they were eventually treated to a lavish lunch befitting such a momentous occasion.

Back in the suite, the Emperor and Empress ate poached Dover sole with *béchamel* sauce served from a *cassolette*, butler-style, using a spoon and fork. As the Emperor was serving himself, he accidentally dropped the spoon on the floor. Without uttering a single word, the Emperor regally held his hand out until his staff placed in it a new silver spoon for his use. Because the Waldorf's staff knew of Emperor Hirohito's visit at least six months in advance, they started practicing correct protocol with Japan's royal household three months before his actual arrival. By the time Emperor Hirohito arrived at the Waldorf, his trip had been well-reported in the press, and the Emperor was met with a slew of death threats from his political detractors. For this reason, his staff kept a careful eye on food preparation in the kitchen to prevent the threat of food poisoning.

Sharing a moment of respect with President Gerald Ford during his presidency, an honor.

Commemorating the historic visit of Emperor Hirohito at The Waldorf-Astoria during the U.S. Bicentennial in 1976.

Posing alongside the fabulous Chita Rivera at the Waldorf's enchanting Empire Room.

Above: During the historic visit of Queen Margrethe II of Denmark to The Waldorf-Astoria.

Left: Standing behind Queen Elizabeth II during her much publicized and highly planned-for trip to The Waldorf-Astoria.

In the foreground as the controversial real estate tycoon, Leona Helmsley, and her husband Harry descend the steps of the Waldorf's 'Frank's Place' on his birthday. Mr. Frank Wangeman stands to my right.

A glance toward Jimmy Carter during his successful visit to The Waldorf-Astoria during his presidency.

Observing Mr. Wangeman's keen eye as he meticulously scrutinizes the banquet spread I organized for our themed nationality dinners at The Waldorf-Astoria.

Exchanging words with Israeli Prime Minister Yitzhak Rabin during his visit to The Waldorf-Astoria, a significant diplomatic memory.

A treasured, signed picture from the extensive kitchen staff at The Waldorf-Astoria, a testament to the hotel's culinary prowess.

CHAPTER 8

Maturity

As I stood before the banner at my farewell reception at The Waldorf-Astoria, the words "from the Waldorf to the pits" seemed to mock me, as if to say, "What have you done to deserve this?" The Pittsburgh Hilton, where I was promoted to hotel manager, was not exactly a desirable destination. It was located in downtown Pittsburgh, which was a rough, industrial area of the city with little culture or refinement. Location aside, the Hilton was a unionized, 800-room hotel in dire need of renovation and repositioning. But I was determined to make the most of this opportunity, and I set to work overhauling the hotel and improving relations with the union and staff.

When I arrived at the Pittsburgh Hilton, in my pinstripe suit and attaché case, I was met with a rude shock. The assistant manager, garishly attired in yellow pants and a red jacket, turned to his bellman and asked, "Who is this faggot?" The lobby was a chaotic mess of seven different colored carpets and outdated furniture, with a musty, dusty smell. It was clear that the hotel needed someone who had good taste, with a European background (like mine) and experience in luxury hotels. Such a person could justify the multi-million-dollar renovation and management changes that were necessary to upgrade the property and reposition it. Though I saw this as a poor excuse for the hotel's disarray, I took on the job with enthusiasm.

One redeeming quality of the task ahead was the unexpected natural beauty of my surroundings. The Pittsburgh Hilton is located in the heart of the city, at the convergence of the Monongahela, Allegheny, and Ohio rivers. This three-river triangle was a unique and beautiful feature of the city, and one that many people outside of Pittsburgh struggled to name. As I walked along the rivers, marveling at the way they flowed together to create one single, mighty force, I couldn't help but feel a sense of pride in my new home.

After 18 months, 2 days, and 5 hours, I can honestly say that I did not regret my decision. The Pittsburgh Hilton underwent a major transformation, both physically and in staff makeup, and I was even able to successfully renegotiate the union's weak position. More importantly, the city itself changed and became a beautiful, metropolitan downtown with new buildings, restaurants, shops, and cultural offerings. The employees at the hotel underwent a positive change in attitude, and I was able to build long-lasting relationships with the union, hotel partners, and new businesses.

As I prepared to leave the Pittsburgh Hilton for the Meadowlands Hilton in Secaucus, New Jersey, I was given a lavish send-off party. But when I looked at the new banner, this time reading "from the Waldorf, to the pits, to the *pigs*," I couldn't help but wonder what challenges awaited me in the Meadowlands in New Jersey. Leonard Stern, the owner of Hartz Mountain Industries, had built the Meadowlands Hilton in Secaucus, and a few months after its opening, he insisted on changing its general manager, seeking someone with more luxury hotel experience and knowledge of food and beverage. I was that person, and I was ready to take on whatever the Meadowlands had in store for me.

When I arrived in Secaucus, at the Meadowlands, I was surprised by an up-and- coming industrial location that was still rapidly evolving. The former swamp and pig farms had been transformed into a corporate park, residential buildings, and shopping malls, and the Hilton was at the center of it all. Despite my initial reservations about moving to Secaucus, I knew that the Meadowlands Hilton was a prime opportunity for me to be closer to Manhattan once again, and to continue my career with Hilton Hotels. So, I accepted the position and moved into the hotel, determined to make the best of it.

But my arrival was not without its challenges. Mr. Stern, the owner of the hotel, threatened to take down the corporate flag if Hilton did not comply with his requests for a new general manager. It was a tense and difficult situation, but I was determined to turn the hotel around and make it a success. And over time, I was able to do just that. With the help of my team, we were able to transform the Meadowlands Hilton into a thriving commercial destination. As the hotel prospered, it played host to a variety of high-profile guests, including Princess Sofia of Spain, Muhammad Ali, and Frank Sinatra. And after nine months, I knew that my time in Secaucus had been a success. But when the opportunity arose to take on the position of Vice President and Managing Director of the St. Regis Hotel in Manhattan, I knew it was time for me to move on. So, I resigned from Hilton Hotels and set my sights on my next challenge.

The St. Regis was a true icon of luxury, with a rich history and a reputation for excellence. As I took the reins of Vice President and Managing Director at the legendary hotel, I knew that it was my job to build on that legacy, and to elevate the hotel to new heights of sophistication and service. I was living in a penthouse duplex in the St. Regis and, at the same time, overseeing an ambitious $18 million renovation. Adding to this stress was a series of personnel and contractual disputes with New York City's infamous labor union, which reached new and aggressive heights during this period in the late 1970s. Things got so contentious between the hotel and the labor union representatives who occasionally threatened me with violence.

One evening, I found the door to my apartment jammed shut. I had to use all of my strength to force it open, and when I finally succeeded, I was met with a grisly sight. Dead chickens, plucked and slimy, lay strewn across my doormat, a clear message from the unions that they were watching my every move and would not hesitate to resort to intimidation and violence to get their way. It was a chilling reminder of the power they held, and the lengths they were willing to go to in order to assert their dominance in response to the employee layoffs we had to undertake. I went so far as to lease a German shepherd police dog—an absolute lion of a dog with whom I became fast and loyal friends—to protect me at all times.

Despite the challenging business environment, the St. Regis, in the late 1970s and early 1980s, was the Waldorf's equal when it came to glamour and celebrity cache. For one, it had an equally storied past: The legendary hotel was built by American business tycoon John Jacob Astor IV for a record-breaking $5.5 million in 1904. The hotel was just beginning to cement its reputation in New York before Astor met his untimely demise, sinking with the RMS *Titanic* to the bottom of the Atlantic Ocean in 1912. In addition to its history, the hotel also played host to an unusual cast of characters: Salvador Dali, his wife Gala, and their leashed reptiles visited the St. Regis during their later eccentric years, as did an aging Fred Astaire and Ginger Rogers. But we had more contemporary guests visit us as well. In the summer of 1981 alone, we were visited by Barbra Streisand, Lynda Carter, Jon Voight, and Gerald Ford—a mélange of scene setters of the time.

One incident involved my girlfriend at the time. On a day like any other, she came to visit me at the hotel and happened to share an elevator ride with none other than Mr. and Mrs. Dali. To her astonishment, the Dalis extended an invitation for her to join them in their suite. When she politely declined their provocative proposal, the Dalis couldn't conceal their displeasure.

Another particularly memorable event that year was the wedding of New York Governor Hugh Carey and Greek-born real estate tycoon, Evangeline Gouletas. Their star-studded reception at the St. Regis was arranged by Hugh Carey's son Christopher, who served as the hotel's Director of Catering, and it brought to the hotel such notables as Mayor Ed Koch, Senator Daniel Patrick Moynihan, and the mayor of Athens, Greece. On more ordinary days, a sure bet for sighting the city's most glamorous stars was the King Cole Restaurant and the Astor Bar, a legendary cocktail bar with its famous mural of Old King Cole, where one often saw Muhammed Ali eating lunch.

One memorable vignette happened shortly after my tenure began, when suddenly, jumping right off of the pages of the Cindy Adams columns in the *New York Post*, there was Donald Trump! And even more surprising than his physical presence, he was requesting to have a meeting with me. But why? I suspected his interest in speaking with me might have something to do with the gleaming black tower he was erecting just a couple of blocks up on Fifth Avenue, an imposing onyx monument that threatened to cast a long gray shadow over the more traditional 525-room St. Regis.

"Do you realize what I'm building here?" he asked me when we sat down in my apartment at the hotel to talk business. "Never mind the St. Regis. This is Trump Tower."

He wanted me to manage his new building which, at 58 floors, was one of the tallest luxury residences in the city. I listened open-mindedly to Trump while he described his project. He was clearly passionate about it, but I ultimately declined the offer, telling him that I did not wish to become a superintendent for a condominium. Although Trump bristled at my comment, we left the meeting at the St. Regis on good terms. It would not be the last time I would hear from him.

Several weeks later, he called me at the St. Regis to discuss Atlantic City, where he claimed his wife, Ivana, who was managing his hotels there, could use some help. On the helicopter ride from Manhattan to Atlantic City, Trump pointed out his various potential hotel ventures from the window, explaining to me where his name would go on each property. The conversation continued in the limousine ride to the Taj Mahal, a casino and hotel, which was built with much glitz and gold leaf. Outside, busloads of senior citizens and other tourists emptied into the lobby and indulged with their coupons in the hotel buffet, along with other colorful guests.

"Why don't you wait here in the lobby? I'll talk to my wife," Trump said. But it became immediately clear that Ivana Trump did not like the idea of her husband hiring an outside professional to manage the Taj Mahal's operations, no matter how costly her solo stint as president was to Trump's hotel business. We left the hotel without having reached any sort of agreement. Afterward, in the limo, I told Trump that his wife did not need me. It appeared to me that she perhaps needed a gofer.

I was glad to return to the familiar rhythms of the St. Regis. It was a smaller hotel but the most elegant in Manhattan. I could preside over every detail there in a way I would not be able to do at a large corporate venture. But the calls tempting me to the other side continued. "I'm going to buy The Plaza, and you're going to manage it," Trump announced to me on the other end of the line one morning. One of those things came true: He did, in fact, buy The Plaza, but before I even considered the position there, his wife covered it in gold leaf, and he sold it again shortly thereafter. Like clockwork, he called a few months later: "I'm going to buy The St. Moritz, and I'm going to take it down, and you're going to help me build the most luxurious hotel in New York." Again, only one of those things came true: He did, in fact, buy The St. Moritz Hotel, now the Ritz-Carlton on the corner of Central Park South and Sixth Avenue, for more than $70 million from Harry Helmsley, whose birthday we had celebrated at the Waldorf several years earlier. But before he could make good on his ambitions to flip it into a pinnacle of modern luxury, Trump sold it to an Australian billionaire, Alan Bond, for $180 million. Years later, in 1998, as the honorary chairman of the American Academy of Hospitality Sciences, I had the honor of presenting Trump with a Five-Star Diamond Award at a dinner dance in Mar-a-Lago. In appreciation, Trump presented me with a signed copy of his book that had a personal message inscribed inside: "Guenter, You Are the Best."

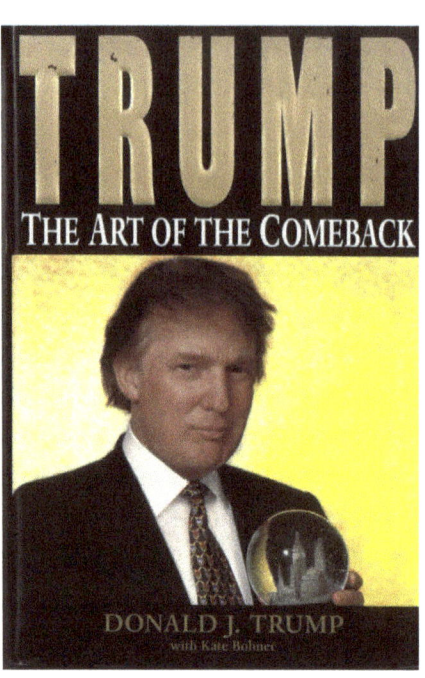
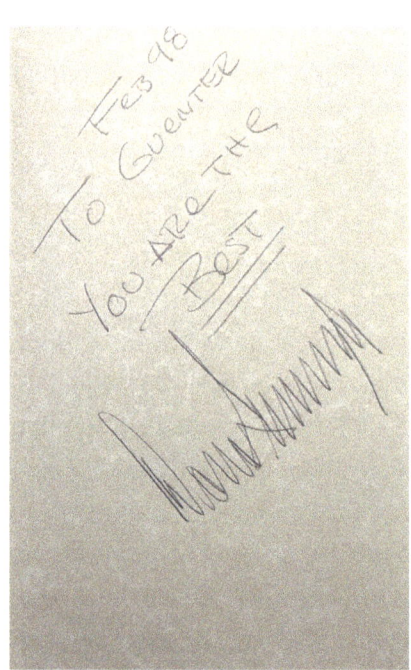

A prized possession— a personally signed copy of Donald Trump's *The Art of the Comeback*, gifted to me during an awards dinner where I presented him with the Five Star Diamond Award at the regal Mar-a-Lago.

I was finally feeling situated in New York again until one day, two years later, Bob Zimmer, a guest at the St. Regis, requested a meeting with me. During the meeting, Zimmer revealed an exciting new hotel venture he was establishing and managing on behalf of a very wealthy family in Texas. He could use my help running it. The venture involved a series of top-of-the-line hotels that would redefine luxury for a very wealthy cadre of clientele in the South and beyond. The venture sounded promising, but I hesitated. How could I leave New York? Sure, the crime rates were high, and the unions had me under near-constant surveillance, but after so much moving about, this city was my new home, and I enjoyed the New York style and milieu. Zimmer, then the president of Rosewood Hotels, insisted that I should at least meet this billionaire family for my own good, and then I could decide if there was "professional chemistry" to pursue. The opportunity to start something new with substantial financial backing was not an opportunity that revealed itself every day. I was on a flight to Dallas the very next week.

Upon my arrival, I was driven to the family's mansion-turned-hotel in the plush Dallas neighborhood of Turtle Creek, aptly called the Mansion on Turtle Creek, to meet the vision behind this new hotel venture and the head of the family. Caroline Rose Hunt was an elegant Texas socialite and, by virtue of being the daughter of oilman H.L. Hunt, was also the richest woman in the United States. She greeted me warmly. Not knowing what to expect from a woman of such monumental wealth, I was somewhat surprised when I was met with her lovely down-to-earth and compassionate personality. Caroline Hunt and I sat in the mansion's garden restaurant where she, together with Bob Zimmer, introduced me to her children and carefully walked me through the nuts and bolts of her new hotel business. The business was a subsidiary of the Rosewood Corporation, a family-owned company with wide-ranging and lucrative investments, located in the Thanksgiving Tower in Dallas, Texas. From big picture concepts to the smallest details in execution, she was all common sense and intuition, level-headedness and grace. Caroline Hunt was not driven by the sheer promise of profit. Her purpose came from a deep belief in hospitality and creating memorable experiences for her guests. I accepted the job as Vice President of Operations and Managing Director of Ms. Hunt's second hotel, the Remington on Post Oak Park, which was then still under construction in Houston, Texas. As the opening of the Remington on Post Oak Park drew near, the excitement in Houston was palpable. And when the day finally arrived, it was nothing short of a spectacle. The grand opening was a resounding success, with the hotel opening on time and on budget to the delight of guests and the city alike.

Houston in the 1980s was the epitome of high hair, acrylic nails, and nouveau-riche excess. The city did not possess the time-tested dignity of New York or Dallas, but I loved it anyway for its wide freeways, humidity, and barbeque. In fact, the social milieu of Houston was no less glamorous than I was used to. Where else could one stay with oil tycoons and royalty in luxurious ranches where bison, buffalo, and ostriches roamed the acres? Certainly not in Manhattan.

One of those glamorous Houston memories was at an elegant dinner party given by the eccentric Baron and Baroness de Portanova. I was seated next to Winifred Hirsch, the wife of oil tycoon General Maurice Hirsch, who pointed to a young woman I had never seen before and whispered, "Who is that girl there, resting her chin on her boobs?" The large-chested woman in question had a wild mane of red hair and a bubbly personality. I did not know anything about her, but I suspected she would be a much-needed dose of fun in a town where I still had very few friends. I went over to introduce myself to Contessa Maddalena di Galliani, and we hit it off immediately. Two days later, we had lunch at the Remington Hotel, two foreigners lightheartedly catching up on the local Texas gossip. I must have made quite an impression on her, because the following day she mentioned me to her friend and business associate, Ricardo Alvarez. A native of El Salvador, Ricardo had studied interior design in Rome and Paris, which made him a truly cosmopolitan and sophisticated individual. "I have somebody you should meet. You will really like this man," she told Ricardo. We did not need to be more explicit than that. She gave him my phone number, and that week I met Ricardo.

When Ricardo and I met, El Salvador was being run by 13 families of which the Alvarez family was one. The Alvarez's were famous for growing and distributing coffee across Latin America and Europe. Cracking under the mounting expectations of a wealthy industrial family, Ricardo Alvarez, then a young man, moved to Houston where, forever a gentle and artistic soul, he painted. Ricardo was ten years younger than me, and within day of meeting him, we became inseparable. Those years were the most fulfilling of my life, and I became close with Ricardo's family, even visiting El Salvador and traveling to Ricardo's family compound in Santa Ana. When I was there, the country was experiencing a kind of civil war, with rebels in the mountains fighting constantly and coming into the cities and towns to instigate fear and murder. Thankfully, Ricardo's compound was guarded with full-time security that provided us with a sense of safety and protection during a tumultuous time. Tragically, Ricardo passed away unexpectedly in 1991, a loss that left a deep and enduring hole in my heart. Despite the loss, I am still in touch with Ricardo's sister, and I continue to cherish the memories of my time with his family.

Houston was the city where I helped establish Rosewood Hotels, and it was where I met Ricardo. But I could not stay in Houston for much longer. The oil crisis in 1984, coupled with the Rosewood's lack of expansion, put a hamper on the business. It would be back to New York with Ricardo for now.

During a board meeting of Preferred Hotels of the World in Beijing, China, with Atef Mankarios in the center, and Peter Bally, the distinguished owner of Park Hotel Vitznau, Switzerland, on the left.

Right: Cherished visits from my mother during my days at the helm of the Hilton in Pittsburgh, her presence always a comforting reminder of home.

Below: Witnessing Frank Sinatra's unmistakable aura grace the halls of the Meadowlands Hilton.

A thrilling handshake with the incomparable Muhammad Ali, who visited both the Meadowlands Hilton and the St. Regis.

Welcoming the elegant Princess Michael Kent, a moment of grace amidst the daily operations of running the Remington on Post Oak Park in Houston.

Caught in a glamorous moment with the iconic Houston socialite Lynn Wyatt, during the big-haired 1980s in Houston, Texas, and my Rosewood years.

Right: Gracing the pages of a men's fashion magazine with my dapper friend and hotelier Geoffrey Gelardi, during our time in Houston, showcasing our shared passion for style and elegance.

Below: Caught in the vibrancy of Madrid—enjoying an unforgettable evening out with Ricardo.

Enjoying a drink at the King Cole Bar at the St. Regis with my girlfriend at the time. We are chatting with a prominent bishop from the Roman Catholic Archdiocese of New York.

Sharing the frame with the charming gold medalist Mary Lou Retton, during the pinnacle of her illustrious career, visiting the Remington on Post Oak Park in Houston.

Above: An autographed photograph given to me by Caroline Rose Hunt (signed Caroline Schoellkopf, her married name at the time) and her children. Mrs. Hunt, the owner of Rosewood Hotels, is seated in the front-right.

Left: Dressed like a proper Houstonite at a party during my Rosewood years with prominent public relations consultant Becca Cason on my lap.

CHAPTER 9

A Homecoming

In 1986, Ricardo and I returned to New York after the close of my memorable and successful tenure at Rosewood Hotels in Houston, Dallas, and Bel Air. Although I would miss the denizens of Houston's wealthy suburbs, who welcomed me into their community wholeheartedly, I was excited to return to the urban vitality of the Big Apple and start the new job awaiting my arrival. The job, which was offered to me by Tom Hewitt, then president of the Continental Companies and Grand Bay Hotels, was to open the first Grand Bay Hotel in Manhattan, at Equitable Center, on 51st Street and Seventh Avenue. At the same time, Ricardo and I built a little home in the Hamptons to escape the hectic life of Manhattan. We enjoyed the summers there and became fond of the winter seasons as well. What began as a Taft Hotel many years earlier soon became the only luxury hotel on the West Side of Manhattan and a member of the up-and-coming Grand Bay Hotels collection, a brand of luxury hotels headquartered in Miami. The construction of the West Side's new Grand Bay Hotel greatly elevated the luxury status of that part of Midtown, Manhattan, which was previously associated with hot dog carts and diners. The location was also the theater district of the city, and contributing to the area's increasingly higher profile were our new neighbors, located at the new Equitable Center across the street. They included Sam's Café, a bistro owned by Mariel Hemingway; Palio, an Italian restaurant owned by Rainbow Room impresario Tony May; and finally, Le Bernardin, owned by Maguy Le Coze and her late brother Gilbert. Le Bernardin was, and perhaps remains, the most luxurious and sought-after restaurant in all of New York City, and with its consistent streak of Four-Star reviews from The New York Times, it remains one of the most consistently highly rated restaurants in the city. If our guests preferred to eat at the hotel itself, they could now make reservations at Bellini by Cipriani, another prized restaurant that further elevated the Grand Bay Hotel as a luxury destination for executive travelers and locals alike.

My return to New York marked another important transition in my career: It was my evolution from a young and ambitious hotel manager who sought out mentors, to a seasoned executive who now mentored younger talent himself. One such relationship began at a meeting for Preferred Hotels of the World, a luxury hotel association for which I was a member of the board. One of the fellow board members, Mr. Charles Kracht, the owner of the renowned Hotel Baur au Lac in Zurich, asked me to hire his son Andrea, who was working at the Hotel Plaza Athénée across town, and take him under my wing. I soon hired both Andrea and his girlfriend Gigi to work with me at the Grand Bay Hotel, where Andrea served as Director of Operations and Gigi served as my executive assistant. Not only did they both become promising protégés and dear friends of mine, they were also two people whose judgment and professional instincts I could grow to trust. Gigi and Andrea soon thereafter married in Zurich, and I later became the godfather to their first child, Muki. Andrea for many years was the chairman of the Leading Hotels of the World and, upon his father's passing, began his role as owner, directing the general manager and his team, at the Hotel Baur au Lac, a Five-Star hotel in Switzerland and rated the best hotel in Europe by Condé Nast. I remain very proud to have helped guide, in a small way, the course of Andrea's professional development.

In the midst of this transformative period, I made another lifelong relationship after I embarked on a sales trip to Europe, where I had planned several meet-and-greet events with potential clients in Germany. Upon my arrival, I discovered to my dismay that the hotel hosting the event had failed to send out the invitations and make the necessary logistical arrangements. As my panic set in, I was informed that Ute Schrader, a highly regarded public relations professional, could potentially save the day. Desperate for a solution, I engaged her services and, to my immense relief, Ute worked her magic and ensured that the event went off without a hitch. This experience not only solidified my admiration for Ute's expertise—it also marked the beginning of a close friendship that has endured the test of time.

All in all, those first months after returning to New York from Houston, with my longtime friend and partner Ricardo, were full of optimism and promise, and I felt excited to start something brand new and enterprising with the Grand Bay Hotels. If there was any indication of how optimistic things were at that time, it was our opening night gala, which introduced the newly constructed Grand Bay Hotel at Equitable Center to Manhattan's well- to-do and well-connected social and business circles. Picture fifteen buff and magazine- ready male and female models serving magnum bottles of Taittinger Blanc de Blancs Champagne to our scene-setter guests, in a lavish evening that embodied the bullish opulence of late- 1980s New York. At that opening night party, I met Pier Guerci, who was the president of the American division of Italian fashion house Loro Piana. We eventually became good friends, and later on, he designed custom cashmere items for the St. Regis, when I returned to manage that hotel once more.

But the metaphorical party that welcomed the Grand Bay to the limelight ended sooner than I had hoped when, in 1988, The Continental Companies, the parent company of Grand Bay Hotels, entered into a partnership with Tobishima, a Japanese billion-dollar construction company that already owned the Stanhope Hotel on the other side of Manhattan. Together, the two companies made an effort to spread the Grand Bay brand more successfully through new hotels to be constructed across select destinations in the United States and Europe. It was supposed to be a promising partnership, but Tobishima was not particularly fond of its new affiliation with the Grand Bay Hotel at Equitable Center— they were of the opinion that the West Side was not luxurious enough. As a result, Grand Bay Hotels relinquished their management contract at Equitable Center, and the hotel was eventually sold to an Italian company, which renamed it The Michelangelo. Because of that, in 1990, I moved to Tobishima's more favored East Side property, the Stanhope on 81st Street and Fifth Avenue, to become the general manager there.

The previous November, just as I was preparing to transition from the Grand Bay Hotel to the Stanhope, a local TV station reached out to me with a surprising offer. They wanted to fly me to Berlin to capture a televised reunion with my family amidst the tide of German reunification. However, the idea of parading our private emotions for a spectacle didn't appeal to any of us.

At the Stanhope, I had the serendipitous pleasure of meeting Joan Koch, who was grappling with the recent loss of her husband. Asha Puthli, the enchanting Indian singer and entertainer, had escorted Joan to the hotel and asked that I look after her for a few days. This chance encounter blossomed into a deep and lasting friendship. A few years later, when Joan married Joseph Sbarro, I was honored to serve as the best man at their wedding. Joseph, alongside his two brothers, owns Sbarro, Inc., a renowned restaurant chain that spans the globe. To this day, he remains a dear and generous friend, and I am ever grateful for the heartfelt bond we share.

My time at the Stanhope Hotel reminded me of the quiet luxury of old New York more than any other hotel of that era. I was even able to teach that brand of luxury to others, at a successful etiquette and protocol presentation in Japan (thanks to my previous experience hosting Emperor Hirohito at The Waldorf-Astoria). But Tobishima eventually fell on very serious hardships, which culminated in the chairman promptly selling its entire Grand Bay Hotel ownership back to The Continental Companies at a significant loss. With Tobishima now divested not only from the Grand Bay Hotel at Equitable Center but also from Grand Bay Hotels in general, it was time for me to return to The Continental Companies.

Imparting knowledge—captured mid-lesson as I taught protocol and etiquette to a keen group of business executives in Tokyo.

Caught in a moment of evening elegance with my dear friend Joan Sbarro, embodying the timeless chic that defined our time together.

Marking the day of my civil marriage to Isabelle Altounian, with Ricardo on the left, and a crisp New York day in the background.

Another image from the day of my civil marriage to Isabelle Altounian, with the city manager of New York City, who married us.

A stolen moment with my dear friend, Ute Schrader, on the timeless streets of Paris during my Grand Bay Hotel years.

A moment of shared glamour with screen and stage icon Cicely Tyson in 1990, during my years at the Stanhope.

Raising a glass of champagne in front of an impressive cake, a mini-replica of the Stanhope Hotel, to celebrate its 65th anniversary.

Immersed in the grandeur of the Stanhope lobby,
a significant part of my life while managing the hotel.

A rare and memorable encounter with Romanian royalty—ex King Michael I, in the hallowed halls of the Stanhope.

My vacation home in the Hamptons, posing in front of the swimming pool in the backyard, a gathering place for many memorable summer afternoons.

Another angle of my Hamptons abode, a sanctuary for lovely, languid summers and cozy winters with Ricardo during my Grand Bay years.

A cherished snapshot from a simpler time: Ricardo and I making memories in our Hamptons haven during the late 1980s.

Right: My dear friends and protégés, Andrea and Gigi Kracht— a bond forged over shared passions and mutual respect.

Below: A meeting of creative minds—sharing a moment with my celebrity friend and Indian artist and chanteuse, Asha Puthli.

Dinner gathering with dear friend Peter Shaindlin, Food & Beverage Director at the Stanhope, my former protégé Jonathan Morr, and Mr. and Mrs. T. Sato, who were key in bringing me to Japan to teach etiquette and protocol.

My second time serving Israeli Prime Minister Yitzhak Rabin, this time at the Stanhope, nearly two decades after my first meeting with him at The Waldorf-Astoria.

Celebrating another milestone birthday in NYC, with Ricardo on the left, and the legendary Pele in the center adding a touch of soccer magic to the festivities.

CHAPTER 10

Tropical Beginnings

The original Grand Bay Hotel, constructed in 1983 with a tropical brutalist aesthetic, was not only the most cherished but also the singular five-star hotel in Miami's old-money enclave, Coconut Grove, at the time. Having already demonstrated my loyalty and service to The Continental Companies, I stayed on with them after the Tobishima fiasco. In 1991, following my tenure at The Stanhope, I was invited to Miami to work at their headquarters.

Ricardo had already been living in Miami for a year before my permanent arrival, and I believed that the warm climate and humid ocean air would be good for his illness. For a year, I traveled every weekend from New York to Miami, where Ricardo lived in a three-bedroom poolside home with his family, who came from El Salvador to tend to him while he was sick. But right before my transfer to Miami was made permanent, Ricardo passed away. I was at the hospital, by his bedside, when he died.

When I arrived in Miami as Senior Vice President for Marketing at The Continental Companies and Grand Bay Hotels, I was met with the wild chaos of Miami, in "storm preparation mode": Hurricane Andrew, at the time the most costly and damaging hurricane in history, made landfall that week, and wreaked a catastrophe similar in scope to Hurricane Ian, which destroyed the state's west coast in 2022 with its Category 5 winds. All the guests at the Grand Bay had evacuated, but a dozen of the staff, including myself, remained in the stairway, feeling the building vibrate, and grasping flashlights just in case of emergency. When we emerged the following morning, the whole neighborhood was damaged, and the ferocious winds of Hurricane Andrew had blasted open the hotel windows and sucked out some of the furniture, including the grand piano from a neighboring apartment building. The damage was so bad that many boats from the bay in Coconut Grove were beached or hanging in the trees.

Ricardo's death followed almost immediately, and the carnage from the hurricane suddenly made clear to me just how fragile life could be.

Despite these initial hardships during my first months there, I became very comfortable in the Miami climate and culture. Miami in the early-to-mid 1990s was becoming a popular cultural capital, evidenced in part by fashion designer Gianni Versace choosing to live there, in his famous villa Casa Casuarina, on Ocean Drive in South Beach, outside of which he was brutally murdered by a serial killer in 1997. That wasn't the only dark side: Cocaine, in particular, seemed to dominate the illicit economy, with stories of its distribution and abuse regularly making headlines. But despite this seedy underbelly, Miami was also a place of great glamour and fame, attracting superstars like Madonna to its sandy shores and luxurious villas. Although the energy in Miami in those years was a mix of party-meets-luxury, it had some serious moments on the world stage to be handled as well, including the annual meeting of the World Economic Forum of South America and the Caribbean. The meeting brought a number of heads of state to the Grand Bay Hotel in Coconut Grove and, once again, provided me an opportunity to apply my experience hosting large and high-stakes international gatherings for dignitaries and important guests.

My time in Miami also represented the culmination of an unexpected personal development that began in New York City, back in the 1970s. Although I am not a particularly religious man, during my Waldorf years I worked closely with ranking members of the Catholic Church, including Cardinal Terence Cooke, the longtime archbishop of New York, who attended many important ecclesiastical gatherings and fundraising events at the hotel. Eventually, I got to know the Cardinal more closely, and he encouraged me to convert to Catholicism. This culminated in a conversion ceremony in his private chapel at the Residence of St. Patrick's Cathedral, with his trusted monsignors as witnesses. Of course, he did not know that I would be celebrating at Studio 54 that weekend with guests of the Waldorf and celebrities in attendance, including Andy Warhol, Liza Minelli, the fashion designer Halston, Grace Kelly, Truman Capote, and Steven Rubell.

Yet the juxtaposition of my newly adopted Catholic faith and my escapades to Studio 54 highlighted an intriguing dichotomy: Studio 54, in its heyday, was an intoxicating blend of sin and sparkle, an oasis where the elite reveled in reckless abandon. Here, one could marvel at Bianca Jagger making an entrance atop a gleaming white horse, or watch as Liza Minnelli and famed designer Halston surrendered to their indulgences.

Beyond the pulsating music and frenetic dance moves, an intoxicating cocktail of drugs, alcohol, and sex flowed freely. This heady mix, combined with the irresistible ambiance and eclectic decor, magnetized a vibrant cross-section of society, each adding their unique color to the canvas of the night. Among the crowd, one unforgettable character was an older lady, whose relentless devotion to the Studio 54 lifestyle led her to its dance floor every day, right up until her last breath.

This kaleidoscopic clash of holiness and hedonism, of the sacred and the profane, spoke volumes of the world I inhabited—a world where the boundaries between the spiritual and the sensual were blurred, and where life was lived in all its paradoxical beauty.

In the years that followed, I preserved my strong relationships with the Catholic community. In 1992, at St. Patrick's Cathedral, Cardinal John O'Connor knighted me into the Order of Malta, and in 1995, living in Miami during my Grand Bay years, I was knighted by Cardinal Giuseppe Caprio into the Equestrian Order of the Holy Sepulcher of Jerusalem, in Miami's main cathedral. This was in large part due to my extensive fundraising efforts, specifically for their children's hospitals. The following year, I was invited to meet Pope John Paul II in Vatican City, which was followed by a small, very early morning gathering in his private summer residence in Castel Gandolfo, a small town outside of Rome that overlooks Lake Albano.

My standing within the Catholic community continued to grow during this time, as did my professional status. Eventually, I was promoted to Vice President and Managing Director of the Grand Bay Hotel in Miami, and all new Grand Bay hotels to be built in Europe. But the following year, The Continental Companies sold its entire portfolio of Grand Bay Hotels to Patriot American, a real estate investment trust based in Dallas, Texas, which held onto it for a brief period before selling it off to Wyndham hotels. Suddenly the luxurious Five-Star Grand Bay Hotel, one of Miami's old crown jewels, became a no-star Wyndham. It was time for me to leave once again.

The jewel of Miami—standing proud in front of the Grand Bay Hotel in Coconut Grove.

An intimate moment with Ricardo's mother, to my right, fondly known as 'Mamacita', and his sisters in my apartment in Coconut Grove.

An unforgettable meeting with Pope John Paul II during a memorable Vatican visit which included the Pope's Mass and an early morning reception in Castel Gandolfo.

Posing during my induction ceremony in 1992, during which Cardinal John O'Connor knighted me into the Order of Malta.

Command central—in the nerve center of operations, my office at the Grand Bay Hotel in Miami.

Sharing a moment of laughter with the iconic sexologist Dr. Ruth Westheimer during my tenure at the illustrious Grand Bay Hotel in Miami—an encounter brimming with wit and wisdom. Known for her frank and often hilarious advice on intimacy, Dr. Ruth regaled us with her unique blend of humor and insight, leaving us with a memorable quip: "You need to talk to your people about the art of arousal!"

Left: Visiting the sublime and icy beauty of the Alaskan wilderness with my dear friend, Ray Velazquez, on a memorable cruise vacation.

Below: Ray and I enjoying an elegant dinner. Ray is not only my longtime dear friend, but an accomplished real estate professional and a court-appointed guardian and child advocate.

CHAPTER 11

A Final Lap of Luxury

I returned to New York in 1999 and was hired by Andreas Meinhold, the president of Swissotel, to serve as managing director of Swissotel The Drake on 56th Street and Park Avenue, where I was also provided an apartment. Previously known simply as The Drake, the Swissotel was more corporate than some other luxury hotels in Manhattan. Fauchon, the Parisian chocolatier, leased space in our lobby, which elevated the profile of the hotel, as did a $4 million investment in Q56, a high-end seafood restaurant and bar. Adding to our allure was the newly inaugurated wellness center and spa, designed to provide an oasis of tranquility. However, the spa was soon at the center of a scandalous episode when a masseur egregiously overstepped boundaries by sucking the toes of a female celebrity during a session. The masseur was promptly dismissed, and to avoid media frenzy, the hotel had to swiftly resolve the matter by compensating the celebrity with $10,000, covering her room charges and incidentals, a transaction that thankfully kept us out of the press.

A similarly delicate situation unfolded at The Setai, Fifth Avenue, during a visit by the Crown Prince. A male member of his entourage, receiving a massage, brazenly demanded sexual favors from the masseur and became aggressive upon refusal. The incident was quickly escalated to the Prince's security team, leading to the immediate deportation of the entourage member back to Saudi Arabia, a country where homosexuality is strictly illegal, leaving his fate uncertain and a clear reminder of the delicate balance required in luxury hospitality management.

However, this was still the era of big corporate hotel consolidation: Swiss Air, the owners of Swissotel worldwide, found themselves in dire financial straits and soon sold all of their hotels, with Swissotel becoming part of Raffles Hotels, a Singapore-based hotel company. Despite the change in ownership, Swissotel The Drake remained a vital force for our executive guests in midtown Manhattan, even though the chairman of Raffles Hotels, a very executive-minded and imperious woman, displayed a superior attitude and little compassion or appreciation toward our team.

On September 11, 2001, the world as we knew it changed: Terrorist hijackers flew two planes into the World Trade Center, leading to their imminent collapse and the beginning of a deadly and costly War on Terror. On that fateful morning, I was seated in the waiting room of my doctor's office, idly flipping through channels on the television. Suddenly, the news alert blared through the speakers, announcing that a small plane had crashed into one of the Twin Towers of the World Trade Center. At first, the gravity of the situation seemed to escape us all, until the first images of the disaster started flashing across the screen. As we watched in horror, a second plane struck the other tower, and it became all too clear that this was no ordinary accident. Panic set in as we witnessed the devastating collapse of the towers and the screams of the victims echoing through the room. When I realized the gravity of the situation, I returned to the hotel to manage and control the panic and emotions of our guests and employees. It had become clear that this was a terrorist attack on America. Outside the hotel, the streets were eerily deserted as people downtown fled in terror from the scene. It was a moment that would forever change the world. That day, I noticed a change in New Yorkers' attitudes toward each other. Usually brusque and no-nonsense, New Yorkers on September 11 were willing to help strangers on the street and stop for anybody who seemed lost, scared, or in need. In fact, many of our executive guests at Swissotel The Drake went to Ground Zero to see if they could be of help. The hotel management stepped up, too. We ensured that the hotel became a safe resting space for heroes serving in the city's police and fire departments. They were exhausted and in need of a warm meal and rooms to rest in.

Having just left Miami's relaxing brand of laid-back luxury, I had forgotten just how much I missed New York. The Swissotel was a great stepping stone back into that city's competitive job market in spite of the real estate difficulties, continued union problems, and a slowing economy facing U.S. hotel executives at the time. Eventually, I was approached by Atef Mankarios, then the president of St. Regis hotels and previously the president of Rosewood hotels, for another opportunity. Atef, who was looking for another Starwood outsider to lead his team (Starwood owned St. Regis at the time), asked me to serve as managing director of the legendary hotel for the second time in my career.

Much had changed since my first stint at the St. Regis in 1977. For one, the caliber of guests and the international profile of the property had changed enormously. Although we had significant celebrity visits in the 1970s, the new St. Regis, after a complete renovation costing more than $200 million to convert the 525 old rooms into 320 new rooms, was even more glamorous and sought-after than the old one. We enjoyed visits from Prime Minister Margaret Thatcher, pop star Elton John, the Queen of Thailand and her massive entourage that kept us on call 24 hours a day, and Hollywood icon Elizabeth Taylor, who, upon arriving late and disheveled to her own jewelry auction at Sotheby's, jokingly blamed her tardiness on not being able to get out of the St. Regis's "goddamned deep bathtubs." At the time, it was the only hotel in Manhattan with butler services on every floor.

During a routine shift, one butler witnessed a domestic dispute between a young couple escalate, resulting in the lady storming out of their suite. She later returned, apologetic and distressed, pleading to be let back in. With no response from inside and her distress mounting, security was summoned. The door was breached, revealing a grim scene: the young man had hanged himself. The situation was managed with utmost discretion: his father swiftly arrived on a private jet to repatriate his son, and the young woman departed shortly after, with the hotel maintaining the matter's confidentiality.

This second go-around at the St. Regis was just as exciting as the first. I was more mature with additional professional experience under my belt, and the property was much evolved from 1977. Louis Vuitton, De Beers, and Brioni leased space in our lobby, and the world's most exclusive guests could stay in many different suites that ranged from $3,000 to $15,000 a night.

But because of September 11th, the entire economy—retail, real estate, hotels, and more—suffered tremendously, and the St. Regis was no exception. As we struggled to regain market share and maintain occupancy, the competition among hotels in New York led to a decrease in room rates and a shift in our guest demographic. Even our most loyal, high-level executive guests took notice of the changes at the hotel, and our esteemed Five-Star restaurant, Lespinase, suffered greatly due to the financial struggles. In an effort to address these challenges, the difficult decision was made to close the restaurant, which led to layoffs and added to the already high levels of stress for me and the union.

Nevertheless, corporate interests came into play again, and tension grew between Atef and the president of Starwood. The hotel's priorities were shifting away from cultivating loyalty, service, and individual relationships, to focusing more on rate and revenue consciousness, volume, and decrease in service and amenities. It was a shift that did not align with our priority of running a world-class luxury hotel. In the end, Atef Mankarios resigned from his position, and all general managers in the St. Regis Group under his leadership were eventually terminated and replaced with general managers who were loyal to the president of Starwood Hotels and had a Sheraton-quality mentality.

It was during this time when I found myself at the crossroads of several intriguing job offers, each with its own set of circumstances and potential. First was from the Taj Hotels of India, which was leasing The Pierre at the time. They offered me the General Manager position, complete with living quarters within the hotel. The opportunity seemed set in stone until an unexpected turn; the chair of the co-op board had other plans. She had personally offered the position to a younger GM from a neighboring hotel. My subsequent interview with her was a mere formality, her decision evidently already made. Intriguingly, the new GM's role extended beyond professional duties, doubling as her escort for various social engagements. His tenure was short-lived, however, and he soon returned to his former position.

The Carlyle also reached out with an offer for the Managing Director role. They, rather unreasonably in my opinion, wanted me to start within a week, an impossibility due to my commitment to a board meeting in Beijing for Preferred Hotels. Their inflexibility led to the offer being withdrawn.

Then came the intriguing proposal from the chairman of La Societe des Bains de Mer in Monaco. He wanted me for the GM role at the Hotel de Paris. But before I could pack for Monte Carlo, he clashed with the labor union there and found himself ousted by Prince Rainier himself! The offer evaporated overnight.

Lastly, there was Alex Hilpert, a man whose dealings in the murky waters of East German antiquities made him quite a character. He had a luxury project in Schwielowsee and was keen for me to take charge. Negotiations took me back and forth to Berlin, but we never reached an agreement. Hilpert, who later faced legal troubles and jail time, eventually expressed regret over our failed negotiations.

I ultimately chose to move back to Miami and serve as general manager of The Regent Hotel and Residences in Bal Harbor, a new venture owned by the WCI Company, then the largest luxury condominium and hotel builder in the U.S. What inspired me about The Regent was an innovative business model that combined hotel and condo living into a single luxury experience, a model which I felt held great promise in the still-growing real estate market at the time. But perhaps a deadly accident during the hotel's construction served as an omen of eventual bad luck because WCI, in response to the subsequent collapse of the real estate market, soon declared bankruptcy and had to sell the hotel before we could ever find out the success of the business model over the long term. Although WCI sold the hotel, the condo remained a successful venture.

The collapse of The Regent led me to my most recent professional relationship—with The Setai, a brand of luxury hotels in Miami and New York. The relationship with The Setai began as my time at The Regent was ending. I was approached at the time by The Setai's management company in Miami, run by Jonathan Breene and John Conroy, to see if I would be interested in managing a new 60-floor hotel and condominium tower in New York that was still under construction. The hotel was owned and developed by Bizzi & Partners and would be named The Setai Fifth Avenue, after its counterpart hotel in Miami. This new hotel, on Fifth Avenue and 36th Street, would be perched south of Fifth Avenue's shopping district, but we were committed to upgrading the neighborhood with the introduction of the new hotel. Like The Regent before it, The Setai Fifth Avenue provided a combination of luxury hotel rooms and condominiums, known then as some of the largest accommodations in New York. The three penthouse apartments were covered in rosewood and white marble, and the construction was so detailed and meticulous that we were delayed for our grand opening in November 2010. In fact, we were still installing artwork and furniture in the rooms when Mr. Bizzi's guests from Italy were arriving at the airport. By the time the hotel was completed, guests could stay in spacious rooms starting at 700 square feet and dine in the new Ai Fiori restaurant, an Italian establishment run by the revered New York chef Michael White.

In the hustle of readying The Setai, Fifth Avenue, we held temporary offices in some of New York's grand landmarks, including the Chrysler, the Empire State, and finally, the Henri Bendel building on Fifth Avenue. One afternoon, upon exiting the Empire State Building, I was met with an unusual number of sirens and flashing lights. A man had, quite unfortunately, chosen to bypass the observatory's fence and make a swift, if terminal, jump from above. Witnesses from above had tried to discourage him to no avail. The incident was handled efficiently and life, as it invariably does in such a city, proceeded as usual.

During the first year of The Setai Fifth Avenue's operation in New York, the crown prince of Saudi Arabia, three of his wives, and their children booked 90 rooms at the hotel, an endeavor that required dozens of changes, layout revisions, and unprecedented preparations and protocol maneuvers. Accompanying the royal family to The Setai Fifth Avenue were dozens of their staff, who worked alongside ours to hand-iron every single garment, prepare every meal, and tend to the royal family's every whim. Because the Saudis decided to come to The Setai Fifth Avenue after leaving the Ritz-Carlton in downtown New York, which they believed was not quite up to snuff, we knew there was much at stake in their visit. Fortunately, the royals were so pleased with our hotel that the first wife princess complimented our staff by stating: "Do you know what wonderful people you have?"

Eventually, Davide Bizzi, the owner of Bizzi & Partners and a man of great taste with a gracious family, sold The Setai Fifth Avenue to Langham Hotels. Right before that, a termination of management marked the end of my time at that hotel. To unwind after my tumultuous exit, I went on a cruise to Alaska with my dear friend Ray Velazquez, whom I had met in 1996 when I worked at the Grand Bay Hotel in Coconut Grove. Ray is an astute real estate professional and also serves as a court-appointed guardian and child advocate. Before we embarked, however, I received a call from my friend Atef Mankarios again, then the owner and president of the Trevi management company, asking me to return to Miami to manage the original Setai property, which preceded The Setai Fifth Avenue by some eight years.

During my time at The Setai, Miami Beach, I had the privilege of attending the 2012 Leading Hotels of the World Conference in Cape Town, South Africa. This annual event, hosted in various global locations home to Leading Hotels, culminates in the presentation of the Leading Legend Award to one distinguished member. I was the proud recipient of this prestigious accolade, a testament to those whose contributions define the pinnacle of independent luxury hospitality.

In fact, The Setai in Miami remains the most luxurious hotel and residences in the city, hosting the world's elite during Art Basel and recognized for those achievements with the coveted Five-Star rating from the Forbes Travel Guide. As the sixth such hotel I managed, it was an honor to be a recipient of this award despite the continued corporate challenges, including the long and tedious process by then-owner Lehman Brothers to sell the hotel, after facing bankruptcy in the wake of the financial crisis.

An engaging conversation with my dear friend Joseph Sbarro of Sbarro, Inc. on the left, and the renowned orthopedic trauma surgeon Dr. David L. Helfet.

A FINAL LAP OF LUXURY

Sharing a frame with the legendary David Bowie during my second stint at the St. Regis—an encounter for the ages.

THE NEW GM

THE SETAI'S
GUENTER RICHTER

After escaping Communist rule at the age of 18, this managing director found his niche in hospitality

By David Eisen

did some interpreting work for Richard Nixon), his path took him to New York, where, for six years, he was managing director of The St. Regis New York. He also had stints with Rosewood Hotels & Resorts, the Waldorf=Astoria, the former Swissôtel New York, The Drake and, before joining The Setai, he was GM of The Regent Hotel Bal Harbour in Florida.

UPS AND DOWNS OF OPENING

While Richter is acclaimed for opening hotels, he admitted it's never the easiest task.

"Some of the developers never hire the general manager or management company ahead of time, so you are entering into the operation when the construction company, architect, interior designer, all already have a year or so on you," Richter said. "Then you come onboard and have to give your input and it may be a different take."

This was the case at The Setai, whose owner, Milan-based Bizzi & Partners Development, tapped Capella Hotels and Resorts to manage the hotel. Richter came into the project a bit late, but most of the changes he wanted were made: embedding TVs into bathroom mirrors (a move that cost $300,000) and adding Duxiana beds, to name two.

"You have to make sure that ownership sees these moves as a return on investment," Richter said.

$300,000
The cost to install TVs in bathroom mirrors at The Setai, a move Richter calls ROI.

The Setai at a glance

Location: New York City
Opening date: November 2010
Number of guestrooms: 214
Owner: Bizzi & Partners Development
Management company: Capella Hotels and Resorts
Managing director: Guenter Richter

The buzz before the opening, the press generating a fervor of anticipation for The Setai Fifth Avenue.

The front cover and inside flap of the book that accompanied my etiquette and protocol training, which I delivered to a group of corporate executives in Japan during my tenure at the Stanhope Hotel.

Mr. Guenter H. Richter
ギュンターH・リヒター氏

30年を越えるホテルマンとして第一級の実績を持ち、昭和天皇、英国エリザベス女王など、国王・元首級の人たちのためのレセプション パーティ責任者でもある、プロトコール エチケットの第一人者。ヒューストンのヒルトン・スクール及び、フロリダの国際大学の客員講師を務める。また、世界中に超高級ホテルを所有するマイアミのグランド ベイ ホテルズ副社長、Swissotel New York The Drake総支配人。

素晴らしき日本の皆様へ――――

　私はこれまで30年以上の長きにわたり世界各国から賓客の皆様をお迎えし、日本の皆様とも多くの友人を得るに至りました。特に、亡き昭和天皇ご夫妻がわが国へお越しの節は接遇係官の一員としての栄誉に浴し、今も忘れがたい思い出となっております。東洋の礼儀を備えた国の皆様ですが、こちらN.Y.でも活動される機会が多くなるにつれ、当然とは申せ、私ども側のマナー スタイルといくつかの点で違いが見え始めたということは紛れもない事実です。中でも「社交」における会話やユーモア、女性の存在の希薄さなど、それが奥ゆかしさから発する日本人なりの個性ということを理解できない者にとっては、しばしばコミュニケーション ギャップの元ともなってきました。

　これらの問題点をお伝えしたく思っておりました私のもとに、ある日本人女性が現れました。そう、MS.佐藤です。すでに一流の研究家であった彼女は、欧米のトップ エグゼクティブの行動美学やコミュニケーションへの考え方を学習し、かつN.Y.における女性コミュニティの場でも、駐在員ミセスとしての自覚と行動を説き、その教室の影響に加え現地紙での定期コラム執筆等、多くの新人ミセス達に希望を与えました。

　帰国後、彼女は日本でプロトコールを広めるにあたり、「できるだけ平明に正しく伝える」「それによって権威付けしない」との約束通り、ご自宅を教室に開放され、まさに伝道師的精神を貫きつつ、この素晴らしい書を上梓されたわけです。

　「東は東」の時代はとうに過ぎ去りました。今、東と西が溶け合おうとするこの時にこそ、プロトコールの正しい骨格とルールを伝えるこの書が常に皆様の身近にあって、国際理解のための大きな一助として活用されるに違いないと信じるものです。

Message

To the wonderful people of Japan

Over the last thirty years of my professional life I have had the privilege to serve many guests, celebrities, dignitaries, heads of state and royalty from all over the world. I have had the opportunity to meet many people from Japan and visited Tokyo on several occasions. One of the greatest honors I experienced was when I attended to His Imperial Highness, the late Emperor Hirohito and his Empress who visited New York and the hotel where I served as one of its directors.

Your country has a reputation for great traditions, particularly in terms of etiquette and courtesy. As more and more Japanese are pursuing professional and social activities in our country, especially here in New York, differences in style and manners that are a reflection of your culture become increasingly apparent. You converse with us in a more formal way than we are accustomed to, and your humor is more reserved and polite. We are in many ways much more casual by comparison and tend to communicate more openly. We also notice that relatively few Japanese women participate in business and social activities, and that when they do join in, they appear less engaged and considerably more reserved than their Western counterparts.

When I met Ms. Tadako Sato I was pleasantly surprised about her eagerness to relate to you the cultural differences and how to overcome the obvious difficulties. Ms. Sato has researched and studied the behavior of Western top executives and how to communicate with them. She has become an expert teacher of selfawareness and prepares the wives of Japanese executive what to expect, how to communicate and how to conduct themselves in our society.

She offers hope to the spouses of many junior level executives by publishing periodically columns in the local newspaper. Herself the wife of a top executive, she practiced her teaching here in New York, and continued to pursue this path with even greater enthusiasm upon her return to Japan by opening her home to instruct and entertain.

By publishing this wonderful book she carries out her original mission with a very clear vision: to convey an understanding of the meaning of protocol and etiquette without an authoritarian attitude.

"East is east" no longer holds true. As east and west are slowly merging, we hope that this book will provide you with a better understanding of our customs which in turn will lead to improved communications and thus benefit all of us.

Guenter H. Richter

CHAPTER 12

Coda

When we heard the first F major chord of Cy Coleman's "Witchcraft," I knew it would be a special evening, especially because the pianist regaling us that night was Cy Coleman himself. It was the summer of 1990, and in the penthouse suite of the Stanhope Hotel, the luxury Fifth Avenue hotel I was managing at the time, a group of some of New York's most prominent personalities gathered to celebrate Coleman's Tony Award for his new musical, "City of Angels." Asha Puthli, the Indian diva and singer, wrapped in an ivory sari and in supple voice, sang special commemorative lyrics to "Witchcraft," written on the back of a menu by lyricist Sammy Cahn just thirty minutes earlier, over a terrine of salmon and lobster sauce verte and a 1983 Chateau d'Issan Margaux. Around the table were business mogul Ed Bronfman, Jr. and the late Cicely Tyson, in a glittering black cap, who had just finished filming "Heat Wave" with James Earl Jones. Real estate tycoons Sam and Ethel LeFrak, philanthropist and socialite Denise Rich, developer Eli Kahn, and actress Ruth Warwick were also in attendance. It was a magical evening. The following Thursday, I received a note from Sammy Cahn, enclosing the custom lyrics he wrote that night and commending us on an "amazingly fabulous party." He even signed off with a little rhyme: "Guenter Richter & Asha Putli/Are they marvelous? ABSOLUTELY!!!" I smiled and tucked the letter away.

As I sit down, reminiscing on the whirlwind of experiences that followed that magical evening at the Stanhope, I can't help but marvel at the vast changes I have witnessed over the years. From managing opulent hotels in Miami to navigating new ventures in New York, I saw firsthand how the hospitality landscape has evolved. The industry underwent a metamorphosis—from the bespoke luxury and individualized experiences that once defined our service to an increasingly impersonal world driven by shareholder appeasement and bottom lines.

In my journey, I've watched hotels rise and fall, both celebrating the success of innovative hospitality models and mourning the decline of those that failed to adapt. Alongside the industry, the world itself had shifted, bringing about challenges and changes that would leave their mark on every facet of our lives. Yet through it all, there remained an undeniable spark, an undercurrent of passion and a desire to create unforgettable memories for our esteemed guests.

As I put pen to paper and recall that enchanting night at the Stanhope, I feel a renewed appreciation for the old-world glamour that had once been the hallmark of our industry. The laughter and camaraderie shared around the table, the beautiful music and Asha Puthli's enchanting voice, and the unmistakable presence of true legends like Cy Coleman and Sammy Cahn, all served as reminders of the magic that can still be found in the world of hospitality.

And so, as I look back on the ever-changing landscape of my career and the industry I have devoted my life to, I can't help but feel a twinge of nostalgia for those moments of pure, unadulterated enchantment. In an age where "personal touch" seems to be fading from view, I cling to the hope that, just maybe, there is still room for a bit of that old-world glamour—a hint of that old witchcraft—after all.

Above: A starlit soiree at the Stanhope—Cindy Adams, Cy Coleman, Asha Puthli, and I sharing a convivial moment.

Left: Another enchanting frame from that evening at the Stanhope, which resonates in memory as a whirl of glamour and camaraderie.

```
                    SAMMY CAHN

                      Thursday
                      June14th
                      1990.

Dear Asha & Guenter -
I would have sent these along sooner but I
had to be Washington,D.C. for a few days,---
In any case here are the lyrics as promised
and I hope they will remind you both of the
amazingly fabulous party you hosted,---
In any case I spent a few days with "our" Cy
in Washington,D.c and we both spoke of you
with great admiration and affection,---
Finally,finally, a little rhyme -

             Geunter Richter & Asha Putli
             Are they marvelous? - ABSOLUTELY!!!


   704 N. CAÑON DRIVE                          215 E. 68TH ST. (4-Y)
 BEVERLY HILLS, CALIF. 90210                    NEW YORK, N.Y. 10021
      (213) 274-7616                              (212) 628-8971
```

A heartfelt note from Sammy Cahn expressing his gratitude for a beautiful evening at the Stanhope.

Asha Putli & Guenter Richter Honor Cy Coleman!

"IT'S COLEMAN!"

Special Lyrics
SAMMY CAHN

CHORUS: (To "It's Witchcraft!")

YOU HEAR A MELODY
AS GOOD AS IT CAN BE
AND YOU KNOW INSTANTLY, ---IT'S COLEMAN!

YOU LOVE THE LYRIC LINE OF IT
THE RARE UNIQUE DESIGN OF IT
YOU SENSE THE JULE STYNE OF IT, TOO

BUT IT'S COLEMAN!
IT IS SIMPLY COLEMAN!
'CAUSE NO ONE CAN DO,
WHAT COLEMAN CAN DO, ---

SO LET US LIFT A GLASS TO HIM
A TOAST OF LOVE ENMASSE TO HIM
AND SOUND THE DRUMS AND BRASS TO HIM, TOO

* A FACT YOU CAN'T DENY
THERE'S JUST ONE SPECIAL GUY
AND FRIENDS THAT SPECIAL GUY, ---IS CY!!!

* AND I SAY FINALLY
AND I'M SURE YOU'LL AGREE
SOMETIMES I THINK CY THINKS HE'S, ---ME!!!

"I DON'T KNOW WHY!"

CHORUS:

I DON'T KNOW WHY
THEY ALWAYS HONOR CY
I DON'T KNOW WHY, BUT THEY DO!

I DON'T KNOW WHY
THEY THINK HE'S QUITE A GUY
I DON'T KNOW WHY BUT THEY DO!

I ONLY KNOW IT MUST GIVE A MAN, -HOPE
HONORED IN A PENTHOUSE ATOP - THE - STAN - HOPE, ---

(Next page please!)

The melody of the night—Sammy Cahn's reimagined lyrics to 'It's Witchcraft,' the perfect soundtrack to our sparkling evening.

My Lifelong Journey of Friendship and Special Relationships

As I look back on my life, I feel immensely grateful for the incredible friendships and connections I've made throughout the years. In this section, I celebrate these extraordinary individuals who have played significant roles in my personal and professional experiences. They come from various walks of life, spanning continents and industries, and each has brought their unique stories, love, and support to my life. Their impact has been truly profound, and I'm honored to share this journey with them.

A

- **Ricardo Alvarez** - My dear friend from El Salvador and the USA, who was my cherished companion until his untimely passing in 1992, leaving a lasting impression on my heart.

- **Isabelle Altounian** - My friend from Basel, a communications executive for leading pharmaceutical companies, with whom I shared a brief marriage.

- **Maggie Archambault** - Trusted and loyal friend and executive assistant at the Stanhope, Maggie was instrumental as moral and logistical support during the time of Ricardo's passing.

- **Helmut and Lydia Asbach** - My dear friends, Helmut was the owner of Asbach Uralt Co., the largest brandy company in Germany, and both have left an indelible mark on my heart.

- **Antoine and Patricia Augier** - My dear friends from France with a fascinating international background, they have been a delightful presence in my life since our days in Miami.

B

- **Davide Bizzi and family** - My boss and mentor from Milano, Italy, former owner of The Setai Fifth Avenue in New York, and a major player in the real estate world with Bizzi & Partners Development.

- **MJ Boensch** - A dear friend from New York, an exceptional executive assistant at the St. Regis during my second tenure there.

- **Emily Bowden** - My dear friend from New York, who served as my executive assistant at The Waldorf-Astoria before becoming Wangeman's assistant and later pursuing a master's degree at Cornell University.

C

- **Ron and Florence Capano and family** - My trusted accountant and cherished friends from Westchester, NY, whom I met during my time at the Grand Bay Hotel at Equitable Center.

- **The Cipriani Family** - My friends and former business associates from New York and Italy, their support has been invaluable.

- **John Conroy and Jonathan Breene** - My friends and former business associates from Miami and New York, who built and owned The Setai in Miami Beach and, after leaving, hired me to lead The Setai Fifth Avenue.

- **Cardinal Cooke and Cardinal O'Connor** - Esteemed leaders based in St. Patrick Cathedral in New York, whose guidance and wisdom I have valued throughout my own conversion to Catholicism.

D

- **Lynda Dias** – Very good friend, professor of hospitality management at New York City College, and my former colleague in the luxury hotel industry in New York City.
- **Henry and Alice Dormann** - My friends from New York, Henry escorted Mme. Cesar Ritz to the Waldorf Towers and we eventually became great friends. He owned *Leaders Magazine*, a very prestigious and glossy periodical for the upper echelons of business and society.

E

- **Bill Edwards III and Patty** - My longtime friends from the Naples, Florida, Bill and I were paired in a cultural exchange program, and our friendship remains an endless source of love.
- **Bradley N. Edwards** - My dear friend from Washington, DC. I became the godfather to his son, Brendan, and our friendship has grown stronger over time.
- **William and Peggy Edwards** - The parents of Bill and Bradley Edwards, the president of Hilton Hotels and his wife welcomed me into their home in Beverly Hills.

F

- **Bill Freeman** - My dear friend from Florida, a former HR director in Houston for Rosewood Hotels who has his own longtime hospitality consultancy.

- **Alex Furrer** - My friend and former assistant at The Setai Miami Beach, who later became the general manager at that hotel.

G

- **Maddalena Galliani** - My glamorous friend from Italy, who brightened my Houston days and has remained a cherished friend, alongside her partner Wesley.

- **Gregory Garber** - My friend from Miami, who sought refuge from Russia and found a mentor and confidant in me during our time at the Waldorf and beyond.

- **Geoffrey and Eileen Gelardi** - My dear and longtime friends from London, with strong ties to the hotel industry. Geoffrey's career started with me at The Waldorf-Astoria when he was just 18, and he went on to become the Managing Director at Rosewood Hotels and The Lanesborough in London.

- **Jens and Joanne Grafe and son Erik** - My dear friends from New York, Jens was Dieter's associate at the Washington Hilton, and his son Erik, from Alaska, is my godchild. Our friendship continues to this day.

- **Joseph Gruner** - My longtime friend and attorney whom I met at the Grand Bay Hotel at Equitable Center.

- **Pier Guerci** - My cherished friend from Italy and New York, who was once the president of the American division of Italian fashion house Loro Piana, and later designed custom cashmere items for the St. Regis when I returned as Managing Director in 2002.

H

- **Daniel and Anna Heischreck** – Dear friends from Zug, Switzerland, with a second home in Williams Island, Aventura, FL. We met at an awards dinner at the Grand Bay Hotel, Miami.

- **Dr. Franz and Liz Hof** - My dear friends from Switzerland, who brought special meaning to my life, with Franz keeping my smile radiant as my dentist in Basel.

- **Dieter and Cecillia Huckestein** - My longtime friends from the USA, Dieter awarded me the scholarship for a general management training program at the Washington Hilton, and later became the president of Hilton Hotels.

- **Caroline Rose Hunt and Family** - The esteemed and elegant Texas socialite and owner of The Rosewood Corporation, who greeted me with warmth and compassion when I was asked to serve an integral role in helping to start her project: Rosewood Hotels.

K

- **KR Kim** - A former business associate from South Korea, who was interested in investing in condominiums in The Setai Fifth Avenue, New York.

- **Frank Klein** - My esteemed friend from France, former president of the Ritz Paris, whom I met when he was an assistant manager at the George V Hotel.

- **Andrea, Gigi Kracht, and Muki** - Our hearts are forever intertwined; they own the Baur au Lac Hotel in Zurich, Switzerland, and honored me by making me Muki's proud godfather.

- **Dr. Hubert Krantz** - My exceptional friend from Germany, who encouraged me to study in Heidelberg and shared his contagious ambition and charm.

L

- **Marta Lacaze and daughters Natalie and Michelle** - My dear friends from Washington, DC, whom I met in 1972 at the Washington Hilton. Marta's husband introduced us, and Natalie, my goddaughter, and Michelle hold a special place in my heart.

- **Christine Laughlin** - My dear friend from New York, she was my executive assistant at The Waldorf-Astoria and eventually became Frank Wangeman's assistant.

- **Bill and Lucille Losapio** - My dear friends from Westchester, NY, whom I met at the Grand Bay Hotel at Equitable Center, when they bought a condominium there and our friendship blossomed.

M

- **Alex Malek** - A cherished friend from Miami and Iran, who owns a glamorous transportation and limousine company in Miami.

- **Dr. Pasquale Malpeso** - My longtime friend and dentist from New York since 1986, always committed to enhancing my dental appearance.

- **Barbara and Johannes Mangold** - The loving daughter of Marianne Willareth and her husband, who I admire for their unwavering dedication to Marianne.

- **Atef Mankarios** - My longtime friend and business associate, who offered me the opportunity to serve as the Managing Director at the iconic St. Regis Hotel, marking the second time I held this position in my career. Later, he offered me the Managing Director of The Setai Miami Beach and vice president of Trevi Hotels.

- **Claus and Dorothy Mazura** - The warm-hearted adoptive uncle and aunt in Germany, who embraced me with open arms, saving me from initially staying in a labor camp.

- **Peter Messerschmitt, Angelica, and family** - My very dear friends from Germany, Peter has been with me since our school days in Heidelberg from 1969, sharing success and friendship across continents.

- **Jonathan Morr** - My longtime friend from New York, who worked with me at the Stanhope and now owns the stylish BondST restaurant on Bond Street in Manhattan.

O

- **Erika and Hubert Oschem** - My loving sister, her husband, and their wonderful children from Germany, who have always been an important part of my life.

P

- **Tommaso Pacini** - a dear friend and the dynamic CEO of the esteemed hotel amenities company, La Bottega, whom I introduced to The Leading Hotels of the World as well as hotel clients in Macao and Las Vegas.

- **Dr. Marcello Persico** - My cherished friend from Italy, who, alongside Dr. Nicola Villano, enriched my life with their warmth and companionship.

- **Hannelore Petri** - A dear and longtime friend from Germany, whose life journey intertwined with mine from Freiberg to Rio de Janeiro to Munich.

- **Pope John Paul II** - Whom I had the pleasure of meeting at a mass at St. Peter's Cathedral in Vatican City, and the following day, at a special breakfast prayer reception at his summer residence in Castelo Gandolfo outside Rome.

- **Asha Puthli** - My friend and icon from the USA and India, a talented singer and artist who has enriched my life with her presence.

R

- **Georg and Annemarie Richter** - My supportive eldest brother, his wife, and their cherished children from Freiberg, who have always been by my side.

- **Heinz and Elke Richter** - My dear brother and sister-in-law from Freiberg, who despite some challenges, reminded me of the importance of family and support.

- **Martin and Herta Richter** - My loving parents from Freiberg, who nurtured and guided me throughout my life, providing a strong foundation for my journey.

- **Werner and Renate Richter** - My devoted brother, his wife, and their beautiful children from Freiberg, who have been an unwavering source of love and support.

- **Al and Monique Romeo** - My trusted friends from New York who have always been there for me, from working at the Waldorf to building my getaway homes in the Hamptons.

S

- **Tadako Sato** - My friend and former business associate from Tokyo, Japan, who initiated my globetrotting journey to teach etiquette and protocol in Tokyo.

- **Joan Sbarro** - A dear friend from New York, whom I met at the Stanhope Hotel and with whom I forged a deep connection, sharing countless moments together.

- **Joseph Sbarro** - My dear friend and owner of Sbarro, Inc., who I had the honor of standing beside as the best man at his wedding to Joan Koch.

- **Gene Scanlan** - As hotel manager of The Waldorf-Astoria, he guided me throughout my tenure when I took over his previous position as Director of Food and Beverage.

- **Dr. Steve Schneider** - My former primary doctor and friend from New York, who served as The Waldorf-Astoria's doctor and provided care for many years.

- **Ute Schrader** - A loving friend from France and Germany, who came to my rescue during my Grand Bay Hotel years in New York, providing invaluable public relations assistance and forming a bond that has only grown stronger.

- **Dietmar and Rosel Schurig** - My close friend from Germany, with whom I shared adventures from our escape from the MS *Völkerfreundschaft* to our new life on the MS *Berlin* and TS *Bremen*. He offered comfort and camaraderie during those difficult times.

- **Robin Steiner** - My friend and loyal sales and marketing director across several of my New York hotels.

T

- **Mme. Tibessart, Werner, Paulette and Stephan Mueller** - My French teacher and dear friends, who welcomed me into their lives like a son, enriching my world with their love and support from France and Germany.

- **Akira Tobishima** - Chairman of Tobishima Corp. in Japan, our business relationship has transcended borders and cultures.

V

- **Reinaldo Velazquez** - My longtime dear friend and companion from Miami, a court-appointed guardian and child advocate and a real estate expert. Reinaldo has been an invaluable source of support and stability in my life.

- **Dr. Nicola Villano** - My treasured friend from Italy, who, along with Dr. Marcello Persico, brought joy and unforgettable memories to my life.

- **Hans and Gonny Vos** - My good friends from Holland, who trained with me at the Washington Hilton, and whose friendship I've cherished ever since.

W

- **Frank and Marie Wangeman** - My esteemed associates from New York, Frank was my boss at The Waldorf-Astoria, holding me to the highest possible standards and serving as a mentor in my career.

- **Sherwood Weiser, Donald Lefton, and Tom Hewitt** - The owners of TCC & GBH from the USA, who have been steadfast in their support and whom I admire.

- **Marianne Willareth** - My beloved and longtime friend from Switzerland, who I met in 1966, and with whom I have shared a bond that has only grown stronger, speaking nearly every day. She turned 100 in 2023.

- **Maurizio Winkler** - A very dear friend who works in real estate in Dubai and was an associate of mine at the Grand Bay Hotel in Miami.

- **Hans and Helga Wohlschlager** - My dear friends from Germany, Hans worked with me at the Hotel Touring & Red Ox in Basel in 1966, and now resides with Helga in Bavaria.

Z

- **Tasneem Zakaria** - A Columbia University student from India and my girlfriend in New York, who lovingly cooked dinner for my birthday during my first stint at the St. Regis.

- **Bob Zimmer** - My friend and former business associate from the USA, who hired me away from the St. Regis to help him start Rosewood Hotels with Caroline Rose Hunt and family.

A Passport to Luxury: A World of Opulent Escapes

Throughout my globetrotting adventures, I have had the privilege to experience and even work at some of the most luxurious hotels. Each one a masterpiece, these establishments have left an indelible mark on my memory, creating unforgettable moments and stories that will last a lifetime.

ASIA

- *The Imperial*, Tokyo, Japan
- *The Palace*, Beijing, China
- *The Peninsula*, Hong Kong
- *The Raffles Singapore*, Singapore

EUROPE

- *The Ambassadore Hotel*, Juan les Pins, France
- *The Adlon*, Berlin, Germany
- *Hotel ART*, Barcelona, Spain
- *The Astoria Hotel*, Leipzig, Germany
- *The Badrutts Palace*, St. Moritz, Switzerland
- *The Baur au Lac*, Zurich, Switzerland
- *The Bayerische Hof*, Munich, Germany
- *The Beau Rivage*, Lausanne, Switzerland
- *The Bristol*, Vienna, Austria
- *Hotel Chemnitzer Hof*, Chemnitz, Germany

- *The Crillon*, Paris, France
- *The Daniele*, Venice, Italy
- *The Dorchester*, London, England
- *Eden Roc Hotel*, Cap d'Antibes, France
- *The George V*, Paris, France
- *The Gritti Palace*, Venice, Italy
- *The Imperial*, Vienna, Austria
- *Hotel L'Europe*, Amsterdam, Netherlands
- *The Lanesborough*, London, England
- *Les Trois Rois*, Basel, Switzerland
- *The Maurice*, Paris, France
- *The Metropol*, Moscow, Russia
- *The Negresco Hotel*, Nice, France
- *The Palace*, Lausanne, Switzerland
- *The Palace*, Vitznau, Switzerland
- *The Palace*, Ana Capri, Capri, Italy
- *The Palace*, Milan, Italy
- *Hôtel de Paris*, Monte Carlo, Monaco
- *The Peninsula*, Paris, France
- *The Ritz*, London, England
- *The Ritz*, Madrid, Spain
- *The Ritz*, Paris, France
- *Schlosshotel Roemischer Kaiser*, Vienna, Austria
- *The St. Regis*, Rome, Italy
- *The Taschenberg Palais*, Dresden, Germany
- *Hotel Touring & Red Ox*, Basel, Switzerland
- *The Vesuvio*, Naples, Italy
- *The Vier Jahreszeiten*, Munich, Germany

NORTH AMERICA

- *The Acqualina*, Sunny Isles, Florida, USA
- *The Bel-Air Hotel*, Los Angeles, California, USA
- *The Bellagio*, Las Vegas, Nevada, USA
- *The Breakers Hotel*, Palm Beach, Florida, USA
- *The Delano*, Miami Beach, Florida, USA

- *The Drake*, a Swissotel, New York, New York, USA
- *The Essex House*, New York, New York, USA
- *The Four Seasons*, Chicago, Illinois, USA
- *The Four Seasons*, Mexico City, Mexico
- *The Four Seasons*, New York, New York, USA
- *The Grand Bay Hotel*, Miami, Florida,
- *The Grand Bay Hotel*, New York, New York, USA
- *The Greenwich Hotel*, New York, New York, USA
- *The Mandarin Oriental Hotel*, New York, New York, USA
- *The Mansion on Turtle Creek*, Dallas, Texas, USA
- *The Mark Hotel*, New York, New York, USA
- *The Palace*, New York, New York, USA
- *The Palmer House Hilton*, Chicago, Illinois, USA
- *The Peninsula*, Chicago, Illinois, USA
- *The Peninsula*, New York, New York, USA
- *The Remington on Post Oak Park*, Houston, Texas, USA
- *The Regent*, Bal Harbour, Florida, USA
- *The Setai Fifth Avenue*, New York, New York, USA
- *The Setai Miami Beach*, Miami Beach, Florida, USA
- *The St. Regis*, New York, New York, USA
- *The Stanhope*, New York, New York, USA
- *The Waldorf-Astoria*, New York, New York, USA
- *The Washington Hilton*, Washington, D.C., USA

SOUTH AMERICA

- *The Copacabana Palace*, Rio de Janeiro, Brazil

AFRICA

- *Sun City Hotel*, Sun City, South Africa
- *Hotel Cape Grace*, Cape Town, South Africa
- *12 Apostles Hotel & Spa*, Cape Town, South Africa

Praise for the Author

"Guenter's ability to connect with his staff has made him a respected manager, and his gift of effortlessly and graciously providing personal attention to his guests has made him a great host. Guenter is a one-of-a-kind personality, with a rare combination of panache, conviction, and good humor."

ATEF MANKARIOS, chief executive officer, Trevi Luxury Hospitality Group, Dallas, TX

"His attention to detail is legendary, as was his unmistakable prodding of employees to always treat guests 'like Kings and Queens!' He has the kindest heart yet pushed his staff to be the very best. Mediocrity is definitely not in his vocabulary!"

ANDREA KRACHT, owner, Baur au Lac Hotel; chairman, Leading Hotels of the World, Zürich, Switzerland

"Guenter is the consummate hotelier and an exceptional leader whose prestigious career is a lesson in the art of service."

LYNDA DIAS, professor of hospitality management, New York City College, New York, NY

"Luxury hospitality is when you feel being cared for. It's about the details one notes only when they are missing. Guenter Richter embodies this spirit of excellency. When Guenter shows up, faces turn to him and smiles shine. In his presence, one feels only moments of lightness and no worries. He always has it covered."

UTE SCHRADER, public relations consultant,
Schrader Consult, Paris, France

"I consider Guenter Richter a close friend of mine. As Bizzi & Partners, we had the opportunity to work with Mr. Richter on The Setai Hotel in New York in 2010. Thanks to Mr. Richter's professionalism, experience, skills, and due to his impeccable management of the hotel, The Setai has been a great success and was also awarded the best hotel in New York."

DAVIDE BIZZI, founder and CEO,
Bizzi & Partners, Milan, Italy

"Guenter Richter is a real renaissance man, truly at home anywhere in the world. The world has changed, but Guenter hasn't. He's always true to himself, forever a perfectionist, and never fails to find a way to make everyone feel good."

PIER GUERCI, former president,
Loro Piana US, New York, NY

www.ingramcontent.com/pod-product-compliance
Lightning Source LLC
Chambersburg PA
CBHW061352010526
44107CB00011B/911